PARALLEL LIVES

A TALE OF TWO CENTURIES

PARALLEL LIVES

A TALE OF TWO CENTURIES

BERNIE SILER

PARALLEL LIVES
A TALE OF TWO CENTURIES

iUniverse books may be ordered through booksellers or by contacting:

iUniverse
1663 Liberty Drive
Bloomington, IN 47403
www.iuniverse.com
1-800-Authors (1-800-288-4677)

ISBN: 978-1-5320-7291-8 (sc)
ISBN: 978-1-5320-7292-5 (e)

Library of Congress Control Number: 2019904015

Print information available on the last page.

iUniverse rev. date: 04/29/2019

CONTENTS

DEDICATION

This book is dedicated to my late parents, Bernard and Frances Siler, who encouraged me and, with complete lack of awareness of their future contribution to the theme of this book, bought a house in 1960 squarely on the Union line of battle during the Civil War battle of Fort Stevens.

PREFACE

But for the accident of birth, any of us could have been born in another time and place. Given the time that man has inhabited the earth and the vastness of the planet, the possibilities are endless. The Civil War is a topic that has countless worldwide fans. Consequently, a book that takes an up-close look at the years preceding, during, and after this great conflict is a subject of great interest to many. More than a few historians have touched upon how in many instances history repeats itself. However, it does not appear that anyone has done a study of the similarities between events of two different centuries, especially not with a description in first person of the events as they occurred. It is only in this format that one can truly appreciate the degree to which history repeats itself. To this author, the twentieth-century, everyday life events are easy to present because I have direct recollection of what buildings exist and contemporaneously existed in the previous century. On the other hand, the nineteenth-century everyday life events are fascinating because of the methods required to learn about them. Specifically, Washington City directories and news articles and advertisements from the *Washington Star* and *National Intelligencer* from the mid-nineteenth century reveal a riveting insight into daily life during that time. It not only repeats itself in the form of well-known events, like the assassinations of Presidents Lincoln and Kennedy, but also lesser-known events that true history buffs would know of and appreciate, such as the existence of a child's game involving a hoop in the 1850s and the hula hoop of the 1950s. The information regarding the nineteenth-century game was also gleaned from nineteenth-century periodicals. Certainly any hundred-year interval throughout history would yield similar correlations.

However, to the modern-day Americans who are potential purchasers of this book, what better hundred-year interval would there be to do a comparison study of nineteenth- and twentieth-century America? For this reason, publishing a book on this subject would be very fruitful.

INTRODUCTION

I have always been fascinated by the randomness of the time and place that we live. Anthropologists' best estimate is that homo sapiens has been a fixture on this planet about five hundred thousand years. Many thousands of human events have taken place during that time, many of which were exciting, intriguing, and romantic. Students of history generally identify a certain era or eras that hold particular fascination for them. If the love is strong enough, it can rise to the level of downright envy of the people who lived during that period. Indeed, but for the accident of birth, the admirer of that faraway time and place might have been there himself, and oh how wonderful, he surmises, it would have been to have so lived.

My fascination is with Washington, DC, during the second half of the nineteenth century. It is only a slight coincidence that I lived most of my life in that city during the second half of the twentieth century. Yes, it is fair to say that I am envious of the one person whose life roughly paralleled mine exactly a century earlier. After all, he had an up-close look at the Civil War and Lincoln's assassination. Of course I had a similar look at the unpopular Vietnam War, the Civil Rights Movement, and the assassinations of King and the Kennedys.

In this book, the "one person" is a fictionalized Bernie Siler, who was born in 1851 versus 1951, and who saw historical and events as they occurred. In that regard, the "I" in this work is the author, who has a fictional mother and father. However, I hasten to point out that every other person, place, or event in this work is real, based on authentic historical research. I have, however, taken some liberty in presenting dialogue. Though this work is officially a historical fiction, it is far more historical than fictional.

Perhaps, then, it is more than coincidence that I grew up to become a lawyer with an office in the very building that once housed the Washington City Hall, the old Circuit Court, and the old District of Columbia Supreme Court, which is now part of the Superior Court. My office was right above the courtroom where Dan Sickles, Charles Guiteau, and John Surratt were tried. Equally non-serendipitous is the fact that I grew up literally on the Union battle line as it defended Fort Stevens and the city of Washington on July 12, 1864, when General Jubal A. Early "scared Abe Lincoln like hell." The fort is literally a block from my house. When reading this work, one will be amazed at the number of times common names, events, and dates appear strikingly close to being exactly one hundred years apart. Then, of course, I glimpsed Caroline Kennedy as she accompanied her mother and brother on that cold November morning in 1963 as they walked with the president's coffin from the White House to the Capitol just off Pennsylvania Avenue, not unlike my counterpart in the nineteenth century spying little Tad Lincoln engaged in a similar journey.

A more recent development that has added more substance and excitement about this work is the return of major league baseball to Washington. When I compare nineteenth-century baseball to that of the twentieth century, much reference is made to an 1860s team called the Nationals. Not surprisingly, like all of the other coincidences in this book, the recently acquired team bears that name. It is yet another paralleled event.

I have tried to highlight the fact that human history tends to repeat itself in both large and small ways. What follows, then, is a comparison of the experiences of two boys growing to manhood in the same city, whose experiences are sometimes indistinguishable but for the separation of a century.

THE FIFTIES:
EARLY CHILDHOOD

1950s

Having been born at Garfield Hospital on November 11, 1951, my first vivid memories began around 1953. One of my earliest memories is being on the bus with Dad to go to pick up a1954 Chevy from somewhere. I was chastised, though not severely, for standing on the seat. Somewhere during that trip, I was shown a metal container on the street formerly used for watering horses, that form of city transportation having vanished not terribly long ago. We lived at 2005 Maryland Avenue NE in an apartment complex.

This was clearly a prominent thoroughfare in the city inasmuch as at the top of Maryland Avenue NE, where it intersected with Nineteenth Street, one had a commanding view of the US Capitol, the Library of Congress, and the Washington Monument. At an early age, I developed a fascination with geography in general and the city of Washington in particular. I would study maps of the city, and I particularly recall tracing the path of Maryland Avenue, noting that it transcended Northeast Washington, where we lived, and took on a separate prominence in Southwest Washington after circling the Capitol building. Indeed, this must have been one of the more significant thoroughfares in the city in years past. From that vantage point, the fireworks of Independence Day were plainly visible. The aforementioned Capitol with its cast iron dome and the 555-foot-tall monument were indeed fascinating spectacles for any child. The bus was motorized, of course, and stopped whenever someone rang the bell or when people were at the bus stops. The latter consisted of steel poles with round metal discs on top that said, "Bus Stop." The ringing of the bell became a self-imposed personal duty of mine whenever we rode the bus.

I loved going to the station and seeing the trains. It had been built in 1907, replacing the old Baltimore and Potomac station, which was the site of President Garfield's assassination back in 1881. The new one was an imposing stone affair and quite impressive. Dad would take me there sometimes to meet his friend who was a conductor on the line from Greensboro, NC. Dad—or was it Santa Claus?—bought me an electric train set for Christmas of 1954. I also vividly remember Christmas of 1955. I received two fairly large-sized army trucks, one for the carrying of soldiers and the other to carry a huge searchlight that actually shone when batteries were available. I recall being down on the linoleum kitchen floor with these trucks at Dad's feet as he ate a hasty dinner in preparation to go to work at the "Pennygon," as I erroneously referred to the Department of Defense headquarters. Later that day, as was the case many days about midafternoon, I would take a nap in the crib that I was quickly out growing. Frequently Mom and I would hear airplanes overhead about that time. I've always marveled at the fact that such ordinary things in my newly discovered world, such as airplanes, televisions, radios, automobiles, and electric fans, would have been unheard of and unfathomable to a young child born one hundred years earlier. Speaking of the latter, during hot weather, an old, gray fan in the kitchen window would go full blast to offset the oppressive heat. One time Dad showed me where a honeybee had self-destructed by flying through the fan from the outside.

Around 1954, the grownups were talking about how some "nationalists" (actually Puerto Rican nationalists) began shooting in the Senate chamber, wounding some congressmen. And then there was the train that came crashing into Union Station on January 15, 1953. A train engineer apparently radioed the station from well to the north that he had no brakes. The station was then cleared, and the two hundred–ton locomotive crashed through the gates and onto the platform and promptly fell through to the foundation. Forty passengers were hurt, but miraculously, no one was killed. The details of that spectacular event were readily available in the *Washington Post* and *Times Herald*.

A few days after the crash at the station, Dad went to work and stayed an extraordinarily long time. Mom was kind of excited, and there was a man on television giving a speech in the cold. Mom said Dad was down there protecting him, whoever he was. Somewhere along the line, it was explained to me that Dad was a special policeman, and that on this day, January 20, 1953, he was required to help protect President Eisenhower during his first inaugural address. The following year, Dad began to measure my growth by that same old television set. Upon that old television we would watch the Redskins and Senators play football and baseball in their respective seasons. But on Sunday nights, the classic *Lassie* would be watched by all.

A Sunday afternoon favorite activity, after church, of course, was going to the National Zoo, founded in 1889 in Rock Creek Park, and then to Stevenson's Pie Company at Pennsylvania and Minnesota Avenues SE. One Sunday, I was running in front of Mom and Dad at the zoo and was warned that I might fall unless I stopped. Accurate prediction. A favorite attraction then was Smoky the bear, an actual survivor of a forest fire at El Capitan National Park in New Mexico the year before I was born.

The church was at Fourteenth and Corcoran Streets NW and known as John Wesley AME Zion Church. I used to look at the cornerstone after the church service and saw that it had been laid in 1894. It must have been at another location prior to that. I could imagine another little boy in the last century attending church in that location.

In those early years, Mom and I sometimes took the train to Greensboro to see Grandma. There we would see all manner of livestock, including goats, pigs, and cows. I would ask my parents why we did not see them in Washington. Dad explained that city ordinances prohibited such animals within the city limits. Consequently, unlike earlier days, pigs, goats, and other livestock did not roam the city at large. Dad would eventually drive the new Chevy down to pick us up. There was a lot of what they called segregation so that on the way back, we only stopped at designated places to eat or use the restroom. This made travel in the South somewhat burdensome for black Americans, but Mom thought it was important for me to get to know my grandparents anyway.

During those years, Mom worked at the Naval Weapons Plant or Navy Yard, as a clerk, one of several thousand employees. Dad was still a special police officer but now worked the midnight tour of duty. So in the summer when school was out, we'd spend our days fishing in the Anacostia River, formerly known as the Eastern Branch, directly across from Mom's office. Dad would explain how to put the worm on a hook head first. He would then throw the hook and sinker into the murky water, and we would wait for a bite, frequently in vain. When the whistle would blow at 4:30 p.m., we'd drive back across the river over draw-bridged Eleventh Street to pick her up. It seemed as though thousands of employees would come out, many of whom were black and women. This was a residual result of the shortage of men during the 1940s, when most of the men were in Europe or the Pacific fighting tyranny. One day while waiting for her, we caught several perch. I clamored loudly for a fish dinner that night. However, Dad declined to take them home for preparation, explaining that the Anacostia and Potomac Rivers were the terminal points for the city sewer system. Later reading revealed to me that underneath the city was a virtual city within itself consisting of water and sewer lines, the product of a massive infrastructural project from the 1870s. A city official by the name of Alexander Shepherd had nearly bankrupted the city with his extensive public works projects, but the result gave Washington one of the most enviable public works systems in the world. This system was the culmination of what started out as a few pipes bringing water from several springs in the northern portion of the city to the downtown area and a few houses having pipes carrying the waste into a combined sewer system or directly into the nearest body of water. This story provided the long answer to the simple childhood question to Dad as to where the waste went when flushed down the toilet.

Every May there was a day during which the public could come to the Navy Yard and board ships and submarines. I recall entering the submarine docked in the river and imagining what it was like to be at sea and confined in such a structure well below the ocean.

1850s

One of my earliest childhood memories is being on a horse-drawn trolley with Father. These things were rolling iceboxes in the winter and rolling ovens in the summer. Father hated them because of the pickpockets. Unwashed bodies and tobacco juice made the atmosphere nearly intolerable. [1] A favorite afternoon activity on Sundays, after church, of course, was a trip to the "Island" to see live animal specimens that had been requested by Smithsonian taxidermists as live models. The Island was so named because its geographical boundaries consisted of the Potomac on the west, the City Canal built in 1815 to the north, and the Eastern Branch on the southeast. [2]

On one such occasion, I was running in front of Father and Mother and was warned that I might fall into the filthy canal. Fortunately, I was apprehended by Father before any mischief could take place. That canal sure did smell bad. Father said dead animals and the product of chamber pots and outhouses were dumped there, not to mention the city's garbage. The aforementioned garbage was dumped near Ripp's Island near the point where the canal emptied into the Potomac River. It was said that the canal had seventy distinct stinks. From the edge of the island near Ripp's Island, one could see a majestic edifice high on a bluff on the opposite side of the Potomac. With the aid of a spyglass, one could see its majestic columns and two oak trees at its entrance. I understood that it had belonged to the grandson of George Washington and was now occupied by the grandson's

---

[1] Otto Bettman, *The Good Old Days, They were Terrible !* (New York, New York: Random House, 1974).

[2] The City Canal still flows underneath Constitution Avenue and serves as one of the main sewers for the city. The eastern branch is now known as the Anacostia River.

daughter and her husband, a hero of the Mexican War. I believe his name was Lee.

Washington City seemed to have several other bodies of water of the same character as the canal but on a smaller scale. One stream ran from Fifth Street W and L Street N southeasterly through Judiciary Square to the canal. It ran through an area known as the Northern Liberties, which was home to one of the city markets that Father and I would sometimes go to. This edifice was a brick affair. Its butchers and other merchants found the stream a convenient receptacle for waste matter. Father and I could take the Seventh Street horse car for this errand. The stream also provided a convenient sewer for the Blue Jug (i.e., the city jail), denizens of the square, and the Washington Infirmary behind city hall. This was the only hospital in the city at this time. It became a teaching hospital for Columbian College. It was a three-story structure with two wings and a colonnaded portico. It had originally been the city jail. When I was ten years old, it suffered a terrible fire. There was a pump behind city hall that some of the poor people of the city and even hospital staff used for medicinal purposes. It appeared to many that the "medicine" was the sewage that seeped in from the stream. There were times that the stream flooded, and it was possible to canoe on Fifth Street. Another stream was Slashes Run, whose source was Rock Creek in Washington County. It ran past New Hampshire Avenue near L Street and through the Slashes, a wealthy area near Massachusetts Avenue and Connecticut Avenue. Many slaughterhouses were built along this creek, which conveniently received their waste. This stream continued roughly along the northern boundary of L Street, and upon crossing Sixteenth Street, it turned north, crossing Massachusetts Avenue near P Street.

The newspapers were full of ads for "legitimate" medicines for sundry ailments. One Boswell who resided on the Island and J. L. Henshaw at 447 Massachusetts Avenue sold a diarrhea and cholera preventive for twenty-five cents and fifty cents, respectively.[3] In 1832 a cholera epidemic had caused many deaths in the city. I understand that back then, the Georgetown cabinet maker William King worked overtime making coffins. Sometimes I would have stomachaches, but not cholera, for which the remedy was stomach bitters. Father searched for a doctor who would treat people

---

[3] Washington City Directory 1858.

of my race. Not having success in this endeavor, he was obliged to send for Dr. J. Hostetter's stomach bitters. The *National Intelligencer* would occasionally tout the remarkable curative effects of this medicine, reciting the attestations of many ostensibly satisfied users. My testament would have to wait. Because of the transitory nature of this type of illness, it was impossible to know whether the malady subsided as a result of running its natural course or if Dr. Hostetter was indeed a miracle man.

I loved the train station at New Jersey and C Street N built the year after I was born, which was 1851. It was an impressive brick affair with a cupola and tall telegraph poles out front. It took up the entire block between C and D Street N and New Jersey Avenue and Capitol N. It had three sheds, which contained tracks that converged and made their way up Delaware Avenue and across the grounds of the school for the deaf. This school had its etiology from an altruistic act by Amos Kendall, the owner of the land that the school now sits on. Sometime in 1856 he heard of five deaf and mute orphans somewhere in the city. He began tutoring them on his estate, known as Kendall Green. A year later the school was chartered and became a four-year college in 1864. Its first teacher was Edward Miner Galludet. I wonder if the college will ever be named after either Kendall or Galludet.[4] If one stood in the front of that station and looked to one's right in a southward direction, it was possible to take in an impressive view of Bulfinch's wooden dome on the US Capitol. Sometimes Mother and I would ride to her hometown at the South to see both sets of my grandparents, who were still slaves. This was near Greensboro, North Carolina. This soon became risky business with the reinforcement of the Fugitive Slave Law of 1793 in the year after I was born. Under that statute, we could have been seized, and upon the oath of any white man that we belonged to him and without the least opportunity to prove the contrary, we could be sold into slavery. As though this statute were not unfair enough for black people, the law went on to reward any judicial officer the sum of ten dollars upon a finding that the person did belong to the affiant and five dollars if he found in favor of the reputed slave. Our trips, however, continued notwithstanding the perils. It was Mother's position that getting to know my grandparents was that important. But even this

---

[4] This college for the deaf and mute, now known as Galludet University, is still in its original location.

courageous position by Mother was compromised with the news of the capture in Boston of one Anthony Burns in 1854. It seems that Burns, who had been a slave in Virginia, had escaped to Boston. However, under that infernal law, his former master tracked him down in Boston and dragged him through the aforementioned process, and true to form, the judge in the case found in favor of the slave master (incidentally receiving his ten dollars), and the unfortunate Burns was returned to a life of servitude.

Mother and I would usually ride the train, and Father would pick us up later in a carriage. The train was a noisy, smoky thing. It was not unusual for the cylinders from the smokestack to land inside the cars and ignite clothing or other things. Each car had a stove in the middle for heat in the winter. In summer the oppressive heat from the outside was compounded by the heat from the engine. After this ordeal, Father would always show up and drive us back to Washington City without incident. It was a long ride through slaveholding Virginia, including Danville, Lynchburg, Charlottesville, and finally Washington. On one occasion it was 3:00 a.m. when we crossed Long Bridge. Father woke me to say that we were in Washington City, though he did not have to tell me because I recognized the 130-foot stone structure that was to become a memorial to George Washington and the unmistakable stench of the City Canal. In the meantime, a half-naked likeness of the first president served as a monument on the east Capitol grounds. It had been placed there in 1841 after a short stint in the rotunda of the capitol. As the floor started giving way because of its weight, it was soon moved to the present spot.

The church mentioned earlier was one of only nine churches in Washington City for persons of color. This was Metropolitan AME Church, founded in 1854. There were forty-five churches for whites. Mother had been a Baptist before marriage but adhered to Father's wishes and joined the above-mentioned church, which was at Eighteenth Street W and M Street N. Occasionally I would see a couple of famous gentlemen at the service. But I could never get a good look at Frederick Douglass and later, well into my adult life, Paul Lawrence Dunbar. A passionate sermon by the enrobed minister was accompanied by a choir behind the pulpit. The men and women of the latter outfit were stern of face and sang with fervor. The ladies wore bonnets and the typical dresses appropriate for church.

The Washington City population in the 1850s was forty-one thousand, of which two thousand were slaves. Nine hundred or more of Washington's citizens worked for the federal government and generally lived in the many boarding houses throughout the city. Father and Mother would always explain to me how lucky I was not to be in the slave category, which I could have been but for the grace of God. But for his grace, even if not a slave, I could have been one of the unfortunate denizens of such blighted areas for blacks as Nigger Hill, Murder Bay, Prather's Alley or Hells Bottom. The federal government had certain buildings that housed different departments. The Patent Office at F Street N between Seventh and Ninth Streets W, the city Post Office on Seventh Street W between E and F Streets N, the State Department at Fifteenth Street W, and the avenue sharing the block with the Treasury Department. Along with the War and Navy Departments on Seventeenth Street near the president's house, these were the principal agencies. The Post Office building, with its several chimneys on top and Corinthian capitals between every window just below the fascia, had achieved some degree of fame before I was born, for it was in this building in 1845 that Samuel F. B. Morse opened the first telegraph office in the country. Its lines were still visible above the building during my childhood.

1950s

I attended Kiddies College nursery school, graduating in May 1956, but not before being required to dance around the Maypole on a beautiful May 1. We all had flowers about us, some attached with safety pins. The next fall I attended Charles Young elementary school near Benning Road NE. The ethnic makeup of the school was almost entirely black. Typical dress of the day was pants with suspenders and a buttoned shirt for the boys and a dress with tights for the girls. Their tights were of different colors. Sometimes in warm weather, the boys would wear short pants, the better for the teacher to fan our legs with a wooden ruler for misbehavior. One day the class took a trip by train to give some of the children a chance to ride. Of course, I was an old pro by age five because of all the trips to Greensboro. They took us to my old friend Union Station, where we boarded a train and proceeded to "far-off" Silver Spring, Maryland.[5] The school was named after a black hero of the First World War, Colonel Charles Young. The principal, old Mrs. Winston, never let us forget the fact that in 1918, when the army said he was no longer fit for active duty, he rode on horseback from Wilberforce, Ohio, to Washington, DC, to prove to the contrary. Boys and girls were in the same class, and it was rumored that the teachers made four hundred dollars per month. Learning was sometimes fun, but the greatest fun was during recess, when we were

---

[5] Silver Spring is now a close-in Washington suburb. In my parallel life, it was a far-off estate belonging to the prominent Blair family (i.e., Francis Preston), an earlier cabinet member, and Montgomery, a postmaster general and a lawyer who represented Dred Scott. The estate, and later the town, were named after the natural formica minerals in a spring that ran through the property that gave off a silver glint in the sunlight. The estate bore witness to the July 1864 Confederate attack on Washington.

allowed to play all manner of games on the playground. Games included dodgeball, tag, a game where players run willy-nilly to avoid a randomly chosen "it" who, upon touching a player, bestowed that moniker on him or her. We also played football with someone's balled-up glove or hide and seek. Occasionally a free-for-all wrestling match would take place. I took pride in being able to use my arms to push myself up notwithstanding the fact that several boys were piled on top of me.

Mom, being typically protective, would always say, "You can break your arms doing that."

Equally typically, Dad would say, "That means you're a tough guy."

Yes, sometimes there would be real fights. I would sometimes come home with clothes torn or cuts and bruises about my body. I was a bit of a daredevil. One time Edward dared me to dive into some rosebushes. I did it. Then Maurice dared me to lick some dirt. Same result.

When these facts were presented to my teacher and parents, the classic inquiry was, "If Edward dared you to dive off the Empire State Building would you do that?"

The equally classic but stupid response was, "Yes!"

There were several songs played on the radio in those fifties years in the category of rock and roll. "Poison Ivy" by the Coasters and "Dream Lover" by Bobby Darren were classics. But my favorite was one in which the little girls in class and in the neighborhood gave me a perfect opportunity to act out. Several of us would take a perch on a street corner and croon, "Standing on the Corner Watching All the Girls Go By" by the Four Lads. I can still see Edward pausing in our journey home from school, and when asked what he was doing, he responded by stating that he was doing what the title of the aforementioned song suggested.

Washington's population in the 1950s was over eight hundred thousand, of which close to one half were black, many of whom were below the poverty level. Mom and Dad constantly reminded me of how lucky I was that I was not among that number that lived in such places as Anacostia, all of Southwest Washington south of the Mall in the area formerly known as the Island, or an area just north of downtown between Ninth and Tenth and M and N Streets NW, known in years past as Nigger Hill.

Every now and then I would come down with an illness that caused upset stomach and vomiting. One such episode occurred on a Sunday morning as I lay in my parents' bed, which had a wooden frame with a bookcase as a headboard. An AM radio was in that bookcase, and on this particular morning, a children's dramatization of *Horton the Elephant* was being broadcast. I will ever associate that story with extreme discomfort. Mom would always call that type of sickness the virus. Fortunately, major illnesses such as polio, smallpox, and cholera were now pretty much under control. The first two were addressed by way of a shot in the arm and a scratch on the shoulder, respectively. The other was addressed by modern-day sanitation, apparently absent in years past. I understood that back then these diseases decimated entire populations. The school periodically arranged for us to get polio shots, and private pediatricians would administer a vaccine against smallpox. When these bouts of virus did strike me, I was taken to a nice man, Dr. Rose, up on Sixteenth Street NW. While there were several men who advertised their healing powers in the yellow pages, Mom and Dad settled on the doctor on Sixteenth Street NW to address my needs. He gave me the smallpox vaccination and was ever ready with the needle to address the virus. I saw older kids cry at the application of the needle. However, after a logical talk with Dad one day, I would thereafter take the needle like the proverbial man. Dad reasoned that it was better to endure temporary pain from the needle than to suffer days of stomach upset. Even at a young age, I was thankful that the quality of life during the time and place that I lived was far superior to that of earlier times.

In 1957, President Eisenhower and Queen Elizabeth of England arranged a state visit in which her majesty visited College Park, Maryland, for an Atlantic Coast Conference football game. The arrangements were made by way of direct telephone communication between Washington and London. They literally had a conversation through the ocean. In this modern age, such international communication was reliable. I can imagine the tenuousness of an attempt at a similar conversation between Queen Victoria and President Buchanan a century earlier. No doubt it was feared that each word communicated would be the last and with no guarantee that the same convenience would be available the next day. The details of the visit and the game were reported in the *Post*, in the *Star*, and on television. Reading those newspapers was a regular assignment at the school. That same year there was big news of how the Russians launched a satellite into outer space by the name Sputnik. As a commemoration, Mom and Dad gave me a birthday cake that year with a Sputnik replica on top.

The fad during the summer of 1958 was the hula hoop, a piece of plastic formed into a circle that was touted as useful in all manner of functions. One could roll it in such a way that it came back, not to mention placing it around one's waist and have it rotate as a result of pelvic gyrations. With pride I hereby report that I mastered all such functions, to the impression of many girls. For this I would have traded nothing.

Adult dress during this time consisted of pants with belts or suspenders and T-shirts as undershirts for men. The latter were usually white but sometimes were sleeveless in hot weather. For casual wear men usually wore an outer T-shirt or a button-down shirt. A variation of the latter included three or four buttons only at the top, known as a polo shirt. For formal occasions, typically church, men wore a suit, consisting of pants that matched a jacket. A shirt, almost always white, was worn under the jacket, with a necktie or bowtie at the collar. The end of the sleeves, or the cuffs, were held together by cuff links, though later they were made with buttons at the cuff. Under pants were generally white shorts, with an opening for convenience for bodily functions. Women's casual wear included jeans or shorts, with a blouse that had buttons or simply slipped over the head. More formal wear included dresses under which underpants or panties were worn. If the typical nylon stockings were worn, a girdle was used to hold up the stockings. If a whole dress was not worn, a skirt with a blouse and a jacket that matched the skirt were used. In all cases a brassiere supported the breasts.

Members of the American League played baseball at the corner of Georgia and Florida Avenues at Griffith Stadium. The national sport had been played on that site since 1892. Even prior to this, the site had been dedicated to sport in the form of a bowling green. Baseball in Washington had begun contemporaneously with the Civil War. It was initially played in a park just south of the White House and then at Swampoodle ground, north of the capitol, and Olympic Field in the latter part of the nineteenth century. The earlier team that had been called the Nationals was the same organization that we now watched and that still officially carried that name. However, when they joined the present-day American League in 1901, they were popularly called the Senators. Another team of the past era was the Olympics. Dad took me to the stadium for the first time in 1958, where we saw the Red Sox play the now officially named Senators. One could drive or ride the trolley to the games. Dad and I usually drove and parked on a nearby street, where some of the kids who were less fortunate than I, as Mom so frequently pointed out, would solicit money in exchange for "watching" our car during the game. This arrangement was never entered into because, according to Dad, they would have watched their partners in crime break into the car or worse.

1850s

I remember May 1, 1855, as a day that we the children of the neighborhood were required to dance around a pole, appropriately called the maypole. What a beautiful day that was in Washington. We all had flowers about us, some of which were attached to our clothing by a contraption invented two years before I was born by some man named Hunt. They called it a "safe" pin. I wore knickers, a shirt, and a jacket. These were topped off by a billed cap, typical dress for boys during this time.

May was also day of bustle, as this was traditionally moving day, a custom originating in New York, a holdover from the Dutch rule in that city. Its origins were based on the fact that this was the day that the city directory was updated. During that time, Mother would sometimes prepare a picnic lunch, and we would go and lay on a blanket near Rock Creek. Around the Fourth of July, we found a nearby hill called Meridian a few blocks up Fifteenth Street and witnessed a fireworks display. We had a panoramic view of the Red Castle of the Smithsonian, which was near that animal park we would sometimes go to. Also visible was the wooden dome of the Capitol and the city hall on Judiciary Square.

In 1856 the grownups talked a lot about what happened in the Senate chamber. Apparently Senator Preston Brooks of South Carolina took exception to comments made by Senator Charles Sumner of Massachusetts, who Father insisted was a friend to the colored. Whatever the comments, Brooks in short order made Sumner wish he had never said them, for Sumner was caned into insensibility incidental to some debate over the issue of slavery. Brooks was expelled from the Senate and fined three hundred dollars for his troubles. But he did receive a hero's welcome in

South Carolina, which included the presentation of another cane with the inscription, "Hit him again."

The next year a slave named Dred Scott of Missouri, a slave state, who had accompanied his master to military duty at Ft. Snelling, Minnesota, a free territory, and had lived some time in Illinois, a free state, sued in court for his freedom. He had been born a slave in Virginia and went with his owner, Peter Blow, when he moved to St. Louis. Later he was sold by Mr. Blow to a US Army doctor named John Emerson. It was Dr. Emerson who took Dred to the aforementioned places. While in Minnesota, Emerson purchased a female slave named Harriet Robinson. While still at Fort Snelling, Dred and Harriet were married and had two daughters. Not long thereafter, Emerson moved back to St. Louis with his slave family, where in 1843 he suddenly passed away, leaving his "property" to his wife, Irene. Therein lies the start of the unfolding drama. On the premise that he had lived in free territories, Dred reckoned that he was now free. He decided to take his argument before a court, where it was accepted in the trial court in Missouri. However, an appeal to Missouri Supreme Court by his owners, the defendants, proved to be successful. Dred had another bite at the apple in the US District Court. He did not prevail there. Finally he took one final shot at the issue in the US Supreme Court. The sad details of that final decision were reported in the March 6, 1857, edition of the *Washington Star*. Father and Mother's reaction after reading this decision suggested to me that this proved not only the undoing of Dred Scott but for all practical purposes, all of black America. This conclusion was further reinforced by the lamentations of many of the black people of the church, the neighborhood, the school, as well as those poor denizens of Murder Bay, on the south side of Pennsylvania Avenue and east of Fifteenth Street W, and of Nigger Hill, an area surrounded by Ninth and Tenth Streets W and N and O Streets N and Vinegar Hill. From what I could gather, the chief justice of the Supreme Court, Taney, ruled something to the effect that he did not even have to listen to what Mr. Scott had to say inasmuch as he was a piece of property and therefore, essentially had no business in court asserting any claims. Because of this, Mr. Scott's arguments did not even have to be considered. Justice Taney did not stop there, however. He went on to further snatch all hope of equality from black Americans, whether slave or free, by declaring that blacks are not citizens and that they have no rights, at least none that a white man is bound to respect. Perhaps the most important, though subtle, message of this entire decision was that, though heretofore, the status of free blacks had been ambiguous enough for some of our class to cling to a notion that our rights were reasonably comparable to that of all other Americans, it was now made clear that our class was virtually no better off than slaves.

Also in 1857, we heard of riots in New York wherein rival street gangs marred an Independence Day celebration. It seems that the Dead Rabbits attacked the Bowery Boys at a saloon. The turmoil continued on until the following day. Because of the disorganization, largely rooted in corruption, two distinct police jurisdictions claimed not to have authority to address the issue. As a consequence, more than one hundred were killed, many being trampled on the sidewalk after falling wounded to the ground. Finally, the army had to put down the riot in the Five Points section of that city, which was perhaps the most dangerous and crime-ridden section of New York.[6]

In 1858, President Buchanan and Queen Victoria had a conversation through the Atlantic Ocean somehow. The teacher said that some species of wire had been laid across the sea. Father had shown me the article in the *Leslie's Illustrated Newspaper* that told how the cable was laid. Apparently the cables were spun on ships that brought the ends of the cable to a point ten miles from Newfoundland, Canada, and fifteen miles from Ireland, respectively. These ends of the cable were to be made especially strong so as to withstand ships' anchors and wave action against rocks. This cable consisted of twelve wires bound together to form a cable of one and one-half inches in diameter and weighing six tons to the mile. At length the vast undertaking was completed. A large parade was held in New York on August 16 of that year in which sailors and others marched through the city. However, before the mood of celebration had completely died down, the signal became fainter and weaker. They say that the saltwater of the sea had an erosive effect on the wires. It was a good thing that the president and the queen talked when they did because this wire went dead in September 1858. By the time I was fourteen, however, a new wire

---

[6] Ironically the seat of law enforcement, the Justice Center, and city hall all occupy that site today.

was laid and was successful. I thought that perhaps in the next century a president and a monarch could talk live through the ocean.

Typical dress among the upper class during the fifties consisted of a black suit under which was a linen shirt, which was typically white. A black bow tie adorned the shirt. The footwear consisted of low-cut boots. In Washington and other major cities, the coats of elegant gentlemen were adorned with fur collars or cuffs. However, the men who loaded ships at the wharf at Sixth Street W and on the Georgetown docks or other working-class jobs wore trousers and wool pullover shirts, along with boots. The above items were either made at home or purchased from a tailor. The clothing indicated a clear distinction between the upper class and the working class. One look at the denizens on the streets around our neighborhood made it clear that Fifteenth Street W near L Street N was a working-class neighborhood. This is all the more reason that one had to be careful of interacting with over civil gentlemen along the north side of Pennsylvania Avenue who sought to offer advice. These men invariably attempted to appear prosperous and could therefore fool one with their upper-class attire. Generally, all classes of men, including Father, wore a new 1850s style of hat known as a derby for informal purposes. The more well-off wore top hats for formal occasions. One was particularly labeled as prosperous if the top hat was of beaver.

The fad during the summer of 1858 was red and black dresses on women. It seemed that only white women wore them though. The men had their own little fad of dying their hair and beards red. There was another activity that an editorial in the *Washington Star* denounced. This was the male pastime of ogling beautiful women on Washington streets. Stated another way, this was standing on the corner watching all the girls go by. We children were enthralled with a game that employed a hoop that was twirled with a stick. With the stick, the hoop could be made to perform all manner of gyrations. I became quite proficient at this art.

During those summers in the fifties, Father would sometimes take me to see the Nationals play the New York game at the corner of Fifteenth Street and the Old City Canal. The crowds would stand around the outer field and near the place where the striker stood. The variety of dress among the spectators was a microcosm of the aforementioned clothing styles, with beaver top hats and derbies worn by the gentlemen. The carriages of the well-to-do were stationed beyond the crowds along Fifteenth Street awaiting the return of their owners.

Other forms of entertainment among the denizens of Washington, mainly among the adults, were oyster saloons, lager beer saloons, billiard parlors, and bathhouses. Certainly not peculiar to Washington, other entertainment for the grownups was spectator sports like horseracing, horse trotting, and boxing. Another form of entertainment among the white people was the minstrel shows. We hated how white men would dress up with black faces and make our people look like buffoons. The show would start out with a group sitting and singing songs like, Stephen Foster's "Old Folks at Home" and "De Camptown Races." Then came the *olio*, the part of the show featuring a variety of performances and then some play that poked fun at current events. When I was small, the most noted of these groups was the Christy Minstrels, who played mainly in New York. A few years later they became the first attraction for a new theatre started by an entrepreneur from Baltimore named John T. Ford. Ford had leased, then purchased what was originally the Tenth Street Baptist Church for putting on theatrical performances. After two and a half months of the Christy Minstrels, it became clear that this would be a successful venture—that is until the building burned down on December 30, 1862. No surprise. When I was downtown with Father earlier that year, we heard the widow Rebecca Gray, who lived down the street from the church at 345 Tenth Street, talking to Mary Jane Anderson, who lived in Baptist Alley behind the church.

Even though they were black and not particularly welcomed at the church, Miss Mary said to Mrs. Rebecca, "That old white lady that went to that church used to say, 'Bad things will happen to that building now that God has been replaced by ungodly entertainment.'"

It was so prophetic that later, Miss Anderson was a witness to one of those bad things from her abode in the alley. On Good Friday a few years later, she gazed "right wishful" at a handsome man ride up to the back door of what was now Ford's Theatre and enter a rear door and also into infamy. They say that the man was one of the Booth boys who frequently acted at the theatre.[7]

The summers in the 1850s were as interesting as they were hot. When there had been no recent rains, the streets were little more than dust bowls. When it rained, the streets were a sea of mud. Under either circumstance, however, they were manure-filled passageways requiring pedestrians who wished to cross to be adept and impervious to dirt and mud.

Some curbsides, like the one in front of that church that later became a theatre on Tenth Street W, had stone or marble platforms for ladies to step onto when emerging from carriages. When these were not present, Mother had to constantly hold her skirt up when crossing streets or getting into carriages to prevent their soiling.

There was one on the northwest corner of Seventh Street W and E Street N near that post office. By 1857, however, there was in place a method to prepare ahead of time as to what the weather would be. In May of that year, the *Washington Star* began to give weather reports. No matter what the weather, however, geese, pigs, cows, goats, and any other species of wildlife roamed at large. For that reason, especially in summer when the windows were open, it was difficult to sleep at night. These animals kept up a continuous uproar as they roamed the city, their owners having no stables to keep them in. They would return to their owners in the morning and evening for feeding and then take back to the streets. Their racket created a perfect cacophony with that of the equally numerous dogs and cats. The owners of the cows created yet another annoyance by milking these animals on the street, frequently sprinkling passersby. Father used to predict that one day the city would pass laws that prohibited this nuisance in the city.

The neighborhood children, including my buddy Crittenden Bayliss, would play games like prisoners base and box with each other until late into evening. Prisoners base consisted of two teams with up to ten children and being tagged or "caught" by a person on the other team and being compelled to stay at one of two bases until released by teammates. The teams lined up facing each other at about 100 to 150 feet apart. In front

---

[7] Indeed bad things did happen. After the fire, Lincoln was shot there on April 14, 1865, and later, after the government had acquired it for office space, twenty government workers were killed when the three floors collapsed on June 9, 1893.

of each team was drawn a safe line. Members of each team would then go beyond the line to entice opposite team members to chase and tag them before successfully retreating to the safe line. If this was done, the tagged player would become a prisoner of the other team. However, the successful tagger was then susceptible to being tagged by other members of the other team before he or she could get back to their safe line. The game ended when all members of one team had become prisoners.

Another favorite game was Fox in the Morning. This game featured two bases twenty feet apart with three children at each base. A six-foot-wide path ran between the bases. One of us would be the blindfolded fox stationed in the middle. The objective was for all three members of each team to run one by one past the fox without being touched by him or her as the players chanted, "Fox in the morning" over and over. If touched, that person would become the fox and the game would restart until one team was successful. There were also games known as The Wolf and the Dog, The Cat and the Mouse, The Cotton Flies, and Blind Postman

We also played checks on green and yellow and red and yellow boards. When we came upon an open field, we played town ball, the New York game. Mother usually told me to come in before gaslights.

The *Washington Star* announced a new bowling saloon on D Street N between Eighth and Ninth Streets W. The boys at school were talking about it because the ad offered a job for six colored boys to set up the pins. When I broached the subject to Mother, she demurred, citing the fact that the ad said slaves were preferred. She constantly reinforced my need to be separately associated from slaves. Speaking of which, Washington City had 6, 521 blacks, of which 1, 713 were slaves in the 1850s. Those of us who were free lived in Prathers Alley, Hell's Bottom, Georgetown, Goose Level, and Murder Bay. These dwellings and neighborhoods featured crime. Once nighttime fell, almost complete darkness prevailed, facilitating criminal activity. A typical police quarterly report when I was around thirteen consisted of forty cases of assault and battery, fifty-nine reports of fighting in the streets, several charges of driving carriages too fast, and numerous robberies and pickpockets. There was even one bigamy arrest during that period.[8]

Another undesirable locale was Marble Alley, and like the previously

---

[8] *Washington Star,* July 6, 1865.

mentioned areas in Washington City, these unfortunates lived in alleys, under leaky tar and felt roofs, and in houses made of cheap lumber and divided into twelve-foot by fourteen-foot apartments. Pools of filthy water were prevalent below the floorboards, contributing to an overall sickening atmosphere. The houses were generally owned by lawyers, store owners, realty agents, and dentists. On the other hand, slaves were kept in attics, stables, and cellars by their masters in other parts of the city. Though free, Mother constantly warned me of the dangers of slave-nappers, including one Stonebreaker, a black man. A lucrative trade in human beings went on in this city, right in the shadow of the Capitol. Not far from where we lived, at the corner of H Street and Jackson Place, stood a house that had once belonged to the Admiral Stephen Decatur and now belonged to one Gadsby. Decatur was a hero from the War of 1812 but was later killed by a man named Barron in a duel at the old dueling grounds in Bladensburg in March 1820. This house's owner also ran a tavern in Alexandria, Virginia. It was commonly known that the attic and ell were used for slave trading to keep slaves and that they were sold in the back lot. It was nothing unusual to walk past that place and hear the mournful howls of those unfortunate human beings being held there. This horrible scenario was also played out at two notorious locations on the Island. They were at B Street S between Seventh and Eighth W and were known as Robey's and William's Slave Pens, respectively. The latter was a conspicuous yellow house. The presence of these structures ruined what was otherwise the only respectable part of the Island. Even the Centre Market had been the site of this infernal commerce until 1853, when the Compromise of 1850 passed by Congress precluded it in the federal district. It was a bit of a pyrrhic benefit in that the trade-off demanded by the Southern congressmen was implementation of the Fugitive Slave Act that was the bane our existence as black folks.

The remainder of the Island, particularly near the wharves, was a haven for pickpockets and teemed with bawdy houses that catered to docking sailors. The wharf area consisted of docks and warehouses accommodating sailboats, clippers, and barges of all species. Respectable denizens of Washington would not generally go there, especially at night, given the rowdy gangs and overall crime.

Other slave pens included Lafayette and Miller's Taverns on F Street N at Fourteenth and Thirteenth Streets, respectively. As much as I liked

Stuntz's Toy Store, I sometimes hesitated to go there since it was only two blocks from those dreadful houses. I feared to chance upon a drove of slaves bound for those places and see acts of outrage upon them. Carroll Row Prison on First Street W at Pennsylvania Avenue also engaged in this infernal activity, ruining an otherwise stately set of buildings. One of the principal routes to these locations was up Capitol South, around the very Capitol Building supposedly symbolizing democracy, and onto the avenue and thence to the slave pens.

These were the occupations of the forty-seven hundred of us free blacks: laborers, shoemakers, waiters, or cartmen. There had been fairly severe "black codes" in effect in this city since 1836, significantly restricting our rights and opportunities for advancement. By way of example, there was a ten o clock curfew for blacks, no black could testify against a white in court, and blacks wishing to move into the city had to be sponsored by a white person. As though to place an exclamation mark on these restrictions, blacks could not swim in the Potomac. It would have been fruitless to emigrate to Maryland for anyone inclined to escape this oppression inasmuch as the codes were modeled after Maryland's 1791 black codes.

We lived on Fifteenth Street W between K Street N and L Street N. The house had a living room and parlor, and it was made of brick. Sleeping rooms were upstairs. Each room had a chamber pot, though Mother and Father had a chair with a hole for convenience of use. Ours was one of the houses that did not have an outhouse. Dirt was used in the chamber pot to keep down odors. In our neighborhood, there was a wide range of inhabitants and occupations. Indeed, this was representative of the city as a whole. There were a hundred different occupations listed in the city directories of the 1850s. For example, some sixty lawyers practiced in the city, as well as several ship joiners and tanners. Among the black people, especially women, there were countless washerwomen. One nice lady that Father would take clothes to at Mother's direction was Sarah Carter, who lived across the street and in the alley just north of K Street N between Fifteenth and Sixteenth Streets W. I remember Father taking her a load of laundry after church on Sundays. The house was entered into from the alley and was structured such that one entered the living room or parlor and kitchen from the alley and found the upstairs quarters devoted to sleeping. Mary Wise lived near her and performed the same services. Made like Mrs. Carter's house and like that of so many other alley dwellings in the city, Mrs. Wise's house was approximately thirty feet long and twelve feet wide. While I have no basis to believe anything of mischief regarding the aforementioned ladies, I learned when I became of age to understand such things that many of the seamstresses and washerwomen found that the wages from those avocations were inadequate and that some, while officially listed in the city directory as being of those professions, also engaged in the oldest profession whose principal places of business were Murder Bay and other notorious locations. Does the reader need any more clues as to the nature of this profession? I think not. Other neighbors were John Gray, a black man at 383 Fifteenth Street who worked as a porter on Capitol Hill. He was in his early thirties and lived there with his wife, Aunie, who was a seamstress. A child who was a little older than me lived with them named Francis. I never have determined what her relation was.[9] The Browns lived two doors up. This was a white family, and the gentleman, Thomas Brown, was the gardener for President Buchanan at the White House. His wife, Nancy, could be frequently seen observing the activities of the neighborhood from her front doorway. They were in their fifties. If they had children, they had long left home.

The houses in the neighborhood, representative of the city as a whole, were either of brick or frame. To be exact, there were 8, 363 dwellings in the city in 1852, of which 3, 080 were brick. Typical frame houses could be seen along Tenth Street W adjacent to that church that Mr. Ford turned into a music hall. They were two-story affairs with horizontal wood slabs forming the outside walls. One had a bay window, likely in the parlor, and the one closest to the theatre had both a first-floor and second-floor porch, facing the street. A little further down the street toward the avenue was the widow Gray, who Father and I would see gossiping occasionally with neighbors.

Another typical set of houses could be found on Ohio Avenue in that notorious slum called Murder Bay. Number 1383 Ohio Avenue was wooded while its neighbor at 1357 was brick. This haphazard mixture of styles could be seen throughout the city. At night, light was provided by tallow tips or a newly developed method of lighting that was born out

---

[9] Washington City Directory1860.

of an oil discovery up in Titusville, Pennsylvania, in 1859. This was a product called kerosene. This liquid substance was placed in a lamp with a wick and lit in a controlled manner. A new company was started the year I was born called Washington Gas company. The public buildings and some streets were lighted that way. Our city lagged behind the Clifton District of Cincinnati, which had gas street lights since 1853. We heard that the wealthy even had this form of lighting in their private homes. Otherwise the only places gaslight was found, in addition to government buildings, were some of the more fashionable bars and restaurants. The principal sources of heat in the winter were woodstoves and fireplaces. For that reason, the *Washington Star* described the superintendent facilities of chimney sweeps as an important official. Most of the houses had no separate room for bathing or eliminating waste matter. Just as in our house, they all relied on chamber pots and wash basins. Water was supplied by springs, wells, and public pumps or hydrants at certain locations on the street in some neighborhoods. Of the former source there were some twenty-five within the district. Fortunate indeed was the landowner who had a spring or well on his property. This added significant value to his land. So valuable was this asset that it was not uncommon for a conveyance and purchase between two parties for the ownership or exclusive use of such a spring independent and separate from the rest of the property. An example of the value of such a transaction in the early part of this century was twenty dollars. By the time I was seven or eight years old, some public buildings and owners of private homes were affluent enough were beginning to receive "Potomac water" or water from the many springs north of the city. The water was introduced into the homes from the river or springs through pumps in the kitchen. They also had pipes taking the waste directly into sewers, which in turn emptied into the nearest body of water, including the canal. The houses that had Potomac water were supplied by an elaborate aqueduct system by Montgomery Meigs, which brought water from the upper Potomac to most of the city. It was started the year after I was born and was not finally completed until 1862. The system consisted of huge conduits lined with resinous pine timber three inches thick, which guarded the pipes from freezing. Its most prominent appearance above ground was in the form of the aqueduct bridge over Rock Creek connecting the city of Georgetown with Washington City. It served the dual purpose of allowing the transit of both foot and vehicular traffic between the two cities as well as bringing in the water. There was a water pressure engine in one of the bridge abutments that pumped water from the conduits into a reservoir in Georgetown. The bridge also featured valves that controlled the flow of water. In the 1850s the service consisting of pumping water from either the reservoir or the springs was generally limited to the neighborhoods from First Street W to Fifteenth Street W in the vicinity of Pennsylvania Avenue, where the water was pumped in from the springs at Judiciary Square and Franklin Square. Because of these springs, Franklin Square became a desirable neighborhood outside of the city. In later years, Secretary of War Edwin Stanton and Senator and future President James A. Garfield lived here. Even later a prominent black senator, Blanche K. Bruce of Mississippi, called this area home. Occasionally, a tank wagon carrying water would come through with a fresh supply of this precious commodity: water.

For those of us who did not have water introduced into the home, part of the household routine, especially for the children, was to lug water in from the street pumps and to gather or chop firewood. As mentioned earlier, the luxury of kitchen pumps was reserved for those who could afford it. For this reason the same well-off people who could afford bathtubs placed these contraptions in the kitchen, where the water and a stove to heat it on were readily available. The Senate and House chambers that were in new wings of the Capitol contained enormous marble bathtubs made of imported marble from Italy. They were longer than six feet and quite deep. I wonder if these tubs will be a lasting fixture in the Capitol Building. I did recall though that in my adult years while Grant was president, Vice President Henry Wilson, who used the tubs frequently, was called to his office for an urgent matter. Without fully drying, he walked in the chill air with only a towel around him and contracted his death. Some claimed to see his spirit walking afterward and hearing sneezing and coughing.

The methods of obtaining water described above were a far cry from Philadelphia, which had municipal water since 1790. The waste of chamber pots and wash basins were simply thrown into the rear yard or in the gutter on the street if not simply toted down to the canal. As of 1850, the city had storm and sanitary sewers dating from 1810, which took both storm water and wastewater down to the Potomac River or a nearby creek or the canal. Accordingly, sometimes chamber pot contents were thrown down these storm drains. But since several houses downtown now had water introduced from both the springs and the Potomac, many people now had water closets. This created the need to provide a depository for the waste matter. Thus the storm drains now formed the aforementioned combined sewer system, discarding both storm water and sewage. With this system the waste went to the Potomac, the Eastern Branch, the marshes alongside them, or a nearby creek. There was little question as to where the contents of these pots were discarded. Some houses had privies in the rear yard, and the owners would sometimes contract with farmers or night-soil men to collect from privies. Frequently our household, in addition to the aforementioned methods, would simply find an open lot to dump the night soil. It was one of my chores to empty the pots in the curb or an open field, pour it down the storm drain, or give it the night soil men who came into the neighborhood occasionally. We had a woodstove in the kitchen and bedrooms. Winter fuel could be either gathered from in and around the neighborhood or contracted from lumbermen.

Most houses were three stories and had a front and rear parlor on the street level with sleeping rooms upstairs. The parlors were frequently used for clergy calls, wakes, and social visits. For families of some means, a piano was usually found in the parlor. In the case of Washington, which was overflowing with boardinghouses, there was usually a tenant or family on each floor or one or two tenants or families in what would have been a parlor if it were in private use. We got a piano in 1859 so I could begin those dreaded lessons from Mr. Withers.

I have described typical housing and home life in Washington City. A significant part of the federal district known as Columbia consisted of Washington County, incorporated as such in the early part of this century. Here fairly well-to-do farmers prospered on estates and in houses that still exist and will likely stand well into the next century. One example of this is the home of Mayor Mathew Gault Emery, who built a frame house near the neighborhood we later moved to. From its double-storied front porches, one had a commanding view of the city. Once we did move to that area, it indeed was used as a signal station for troops occupying nearby Forts Totten, Slocum, DeRussey, and Massachusetts, which was being constructed shortly after we moved there. There was also Mr. Benedict Jost, a Swiss immigrant who ran a hotel downtown. He later became a merchant of fine wines doing business at 131 Pennsylvania Avenue at Seventeenth Street W. Having obviously been successful in his business concern, he then purchased a farm in Brightwood, near Vinegar Hill. When we moved to the latter place in 1860, he had been there for a year. It was a brick affair also with a southward orientation toward the city. In the first years of his ownership, he and his family continued to live downtown, offering the house for rent as a new first-class brick house for a fashionable family. It was obviously one of the first outlying houses to be supplied with Potomac water or some nearby spring water since Mr. Jost offered nine rooms, including a bathroom.[10]

I will subsequently summarize the demographics of Vinegar Hill. One of the free black denizens was Mrs. Elizabeth Proctor Thomas, affectionately known by us children, and adults too, as Aunt Betty. Her case was a particularly disturbing one insofar as the way the government seized private land for military purposes. This practice was typical, as in the case of county road supervisor B. T. Swart, whose land was taken for the construction of Fort DeRussey in our neighborhood. It is rumored that his claims for compensation by the government have been repeatedly rejected. Colonel Jehiel Brooks in the eastern part of the county endured the same experience at the hands of the government. The unsympathetic attitude displayed by the government to these relatively wealthy landowners had an even more devastating effect when applied to those of more meager means, like Aunt Betty. She had bought the farm in 1840 and worked it up until the great rebellion. I remember the demolition of the house and barn outbuildings from our house nearby. Then came the construction of rifle pits and the magazine over what had been her cellar as soldiers and enslaved people toiled sometimes to the strains of the "Battle Cry of Freedom."

As I became an adult, oldsters in the area still continued to say, "Aunt Betty still ain't got paid."

Notwithstanding this description of the plight of these homeowners when war came, these were typical of the styles of homes and their owners outside Washington City. Maybe by 1904 she will. Back in the city,

---

[10] Kim Williams, *Lost Farms and Estates* (Charleston, South Carolina: The History Press, 2018).

there was only one paved street gutter during the 1850s, and that was on Pennsylvania Avenue. In many houses, garbage and trash joined the waste matter in the yard or street. Aside from the general appearance of a neighborhood, it was also possible to determine the social status of the occupants of a house by the species of garbage found in their yards. Generally the wealthy's yards were filled with the bones of cattle, swine, or rare species of fowl. Some houses had a drain leading from the rear yard across the sidewalk and into the street. This conduit was no more than a less-exertive means to accomplish the same task of dumping waste matter into the street. These methods were the closest Washington City had to the sewers that were now coming into use in Philadelphia and New York. In those cities as well as in Boston, we heard that there were fancy apartment hotels like the Hotel Pelham in Boston that boasted heated municipal water and water closets that carried out waste water into a sewer system.

I heard that at about the time I was seven, down at the Capitol building, the senators had something called flush toilets and bathtubs. I did ask Father where the waste went from the so-called flushing water closets in the White House and the Senate chamber. Father's reply was that as far as he knew, it went into the old canal, a spring, the Potomac, or the nearest body of water. As early as the 1830s I understand that President Van Buren had one of those tubs in the president's house. Currently in the president's house there were at least two water closets off the president's bedroom and his office respectively. For the rest of us everyday people, black and white, the facilities were fairly primitive. Bathing in a tin bathtub with water heated on a woodstove was the norm. There were occasionally advertisements in the *Star* by a plumbing shop on Sixth Street W near that big courthouse for the sale of all manner of water closets and bathtubs. It was at 487 Sixth Street and kept "constantly on hand" bathtubs, water closets, wash hand basins, galvanized, block tin, and earthen water pipes for introduction of Potomac water. This referred to the water from Mr. Meigs's aqueduct that conveyed river water from up the river to the city. Indeed if one could afford it, a complete bathroom could be put in with wooden pipes bringing water into the house as was the case with the Lomax family on G Street N. Of those who had water but not a complete bathroom, many had the aforementioned bathtub in the kitchen. The closest we came to this wealth was when Father obtained a chair with a hole in it so we could conveniently use the chamber pot. Our house was lighted by kerosene lamps and heated by woodstoves, and bathing was done in a tin tub in the kitchen.

Overall Washington City was described in less-than-flattering terms by observers. A congressman Albert Riddle of Ohio described Pennsylvania Avenue as poorly paved with cobblestone and twelve rods wide. Other streets were described as deserts of dust, sand, and mud, having poorly built houses with long gaps between them. The street boundaries were undefined and eventually led into a wilderness.

When Father did not go to the northern liberties market, Mother, along with many other ladies, would go to the Centre Market on Pennsylvania Avenue between Seventh and Ninth Street W to obtain our food. This complex consisted of four white shelters, one of which fronted on the canal. This made a convenient dumping place for the garbage that was inevitably collected. Two other shelters were adjacent to Pennsylvania and Louisiana Avenues, running diagonally to northeast and northwest respectively. The former street was the sight of rather comical scenes as trolley drivers would frequently be retarded in their progress by the many customers, geese, pigs, and horse carts in and around the market. The frustrated chap would invariably yell and curse until the way was clear.

In August of 1857, the *Washington Star* provided a list of prices advertised at the market as follows:[11]

- Beef: Ten cents and fifteen cents per pound
- Pork and mutton: Twelve cents and fifteen cents per pound
- Crabs: Twenty-five cents per dozen
- Terrapins: Thirty-seven cents and eighty-seven cents each

Sometimes eliminating a need for a trip to the market were the ever-present hucksters who roamed up and down neighborhood streets crying about oysters and fruit for sale. Whether obtained from the hucksters or the markets, food, and meat in particular, had an underlying malady. That malady was the likelihood that the food would be tainted. While on display pending sale, no effort was made to preserve it, though methods of preservation did exist. Typically springs and icehouses served this purpose

---

[11] Brochet, *Alley Life in Washington* (Chicago: University of Chicago Press, 1980).

and were generally found at the homes of the more opulent citizens but not found at the markets. To make the best decision insofar as which meat to purchase, the sophisticated smell test was applied. Among the poor, there was little or no choice notwithstanding the outcome of the test. After making the best decision possible as to the freshness of the meat, Mother would engage in the art of preservation by an alternate method. It was a familiar and pleasurable sound, knowing that good food was forthcoming, to hear Mother pounding a fish flat with a wooden block or some similar device, the fish then being hung in the sun until it was ready to prepare. She would cut other meats into small pieces and salt them. Thus we managed to remain clear of the illnesses associated with the consumption of tainted food. Folks who lived in the countryside addressed this problem by turning to fruits and vegetables. This strategy was not prevalent in the city since it was widely believed that earlier outbreaks of cholera in Washington, New Orleans, and other cities earlier in the century were attributable to tainted fruits and vegetables.

Although these were the items whose prices were listed in the paper, this was not necessarily typical fare for average Americans at this time, especially black folks. For dinner Mother would typically prepare fried ham with red-eyed gravy with bread or biscuits on our woodstove. Other meats would be cooked at times, such as beef and pork, after having preserved them by the aforementioned methods. Some of the wealthy people would eat expensive fowl like pigeon and partridge and usually some vegetable like peas, lettuce, or beans. Sometimes these vegetables were obtained for one of the markets or as was typical among many Washingtonians these were grown in gardens. Lemonade, water, or tea would be our drink. If my behavior had been described as particularly good, I could sometimes expect the treat of sarsaparilla. However, generally that was a hard standard to meet given the general lack of sensitivity to children's feelings or viewpoints that was prevalent in nineteenth-century America. In cold weather, Mother would frequently make soup or a stew consisting of bacon, peas, beans, and red pepper. To complement this soul-warming meal was the hot drink hopping john. Mother and Father would frequently drink hot coffee. When we ate the meat, Lea and Perrin's Worcestershire Sauce, which had been around since 1835, made the meat even tastier. A quick meal could be found in the form of Underwood's deviled ham in a can, a product that had been around since 1822.

The Centre Market could also reasonably be described as the social gathering place for the city. Persons wishing to arrange a downtown rendezvous would frequently use this location as the meeting place. It appeared that if there was one public setting in the city that defied class distinctions, it was this market. The poor as well as the well-to-do mingled as they bargained for fresh produce. On one errand there, I heard an adult whisper and point to Dolly Madison, a grand old lady in the dress of my grandmother and who still lived in the city where she became famous. That fame derived from her bravery in the face of the British invasion of 1814 while she was the first lady. As a rule, however, we black folks would be given great pause before meeting there inasmuch as in years past, many of us met there quite involuntarily. The market had been frequently used as a slave-trading location.

On the other side of Pennsylvania Avenue were such firms as harness makers, stove factories, and ice cream parlors between Seventh and Twelfth Streets W. The latter concerns were frequent stops on Sundays after church. It was on this side of the avenue that there was a brick sidewalk and the genteel promenaded late afternoons. The "genteel" consisted of congressmen, statesmen, and businessmen. Mixed in with that illustrious crowd were the ever-persistent confidence men whispering and grabbing elbows, vendors and hucksters shouting their wares, along with pickpockets.

By contrast, the side of the avenue where the Centre Market was located was populated with seedy rooming houses, like those of Mrs. Rolfe and Mrs. Scott's. Seediness was measured on a sliding price scale from three dollars to ten dollars per night, corresponding to most seedy to least seedy. Thrown in the mix were gambling establishments, like the Palace of Fortune between Fifth and Sixth Streets W and the ever-present canterburies, which were concentrated between Twelfth and Thirteenth Streets W. Within those walls men engaged in throwing the papers for money and birdcage, or throwing dice. Notorious among these was a row of gambling places on the north side of E Street N adjacent to Grover's Theatre and across from Willard's Hotel.

Washington City and the city of Georgetown had fifteen academies for the education of black children. These were the progeny of the first black schoolhouse built for blacks in 1807 by three former slaves. Father could never understand why he had to pay taxes for the Washington public schools but had to find an academy for me. Accordingly, public schools were not an option for me, nor was the prestigious Rittenhouse Academy on Indiana Avenue, nor the public schools run by Mrs. Cox and Mrs. Marlot, respectively. Because of Father's efforts, the public schools benefited as evidenced by the Fourth of July 1864 dedication of the Wallach School named after a former mayor. It was complete with ventilation shafts, covered walkways to the outhouses, and a furnace for heat in winter. It was located on D Street S between Seventh and Eighth Street E. This school had an oval carriageway in front with a fountain in the middle of the oval. There were trees on either side of the entrance that featured three arched doorways.

The public school system in the 1850s was divided into several school districts that served one or more wards. There were usually two grammar schools, two intermediate schools, two to four primary schools, and several secondary schools. Some of these schools were male or female or contained male and female departments. There was a teacher assigned to each school department.

The academies for blacks were run by churches, relief societies, missionaries, and individual persons: anyone besides the government that Father was paying taxes to. Fortunately, by the time I started school, a white lady from New York named Mrytilla Miner had started a black school on N Street N the year I was born at the corner of Twentieth Street W. The school was structured such that it taught young women of color primary education and domestic skills. Could it be that future generations of our race would have teachers of color teaching in the city school system? Indeed this was Miss Miner's hope as well as that of the members of our race. Mother was supposed to go, but the white people kept making her move the school.[12]

Even the mayor, Walter Lenox, had said that the school might educate

---

[12] When the author was a child, roughly a hundred years after Miss Miner's venture in 1962, his mother received her teaching credential at a progeny of Miss Minor's school, Miner Teachers College, now DC Teachers College and part of the University of the District of Columbia.

blacks "far beyond what their political and social conditions justify." In 1862, someone in Congress must have heard some of Father's complaints. In that year a law was passed in which 10 percent of the taxes collected from blacks in Washington had to go for the establishment of a public school for their children. This also led to the establishment of a board of trustees for colored schools of Washington. Notwithstanding this effort, only one teacher was hired, and no schools were built immediately. As it turned out, no superintendent for these schools would be appointed until 1872. He was entitled the superintendent of colored schools for Washington and Georgetown. Not until 1877 was there a secondary school graduation in the United States for black children.

Flying in the face of Mayor Lenox's logic was the proficiency that I acquired on the piano through the lessons Mother had arranged with a white man by the name of Withers. He was a stout, broad-necked man with a handlebar mustache.[13] He taught music at his house on Sixth Street E, which was not far from the location of that newly planned college for the deaf and mute. This campus was designed by Frederick Law Olmstead, who had designed New York's Central Park in 1857 and the grounds of the United States Capitol. Also the railway that led from the B and O Station at New Jersey Avenue and C Streets traversed the southeast edge of those grounds. He placed winding carriageways as well as gas lamps on the grounds. No less a contradiction to the theory that people of my race were unable to learn was "Blind Tom," a child prodigy of unbelievable musical talents. Born a couple of years before me as a slave, his talents were displayed by his master in concerts that resulted in tremendous profits, of which Tom had no share. In early June 1860, he played for President Buchanan at the White House. Mother kept using him as an example of how good I could be if I but applied myself. Somehow, at age eight, it

---

[13] William Withers taught music from his home at 545 Sixth Street E. He gained some notoriety later on April 14, 1865, as he was chased from the stage of Ford's Theater by a crazed actor who charged across the stage, slashing Withers's coat with a dagger. It was first thought by some of the seventeen hundred people in the theatre that the actor was somehow part of the performance. Fairly quickly thereafter it became apparent that this actor was in his final and most notorious performance, bungling it just as he had his first. More details of this performance will be presented later.

appeared that one would first have to be blind and second, be a slave to be that good. No thank you.[14]

Mr. Withers would sometimes speak of another boy who was a little younger than I who was quite a musician. Unlike Blind Tom, he was neither black nor blind. His father was named Antonio and was a member of the Marine Corps band. The boy must have taken lessons somewhere else because I never saw him at Mr. Withers's house, but I saw him later in May of 1865 as the both of us stood fascinated at the endless stream of that marked a great military victory celebration on Pennsylvania Avenue. He was about eleven then and I was thirteen as the bands played among other songs,

"Tramp, Tramp, Tramp the boys are marching. cheer up, comrades, they will come."

He was apparently quite good at an early age. His family lived at 318 B Street S. Later during adulthood I heard his name again, and I suppose he had become quite famous. It appears that he joined the Marine Corps Band at age fourteen, where his father already played trombone and when he grew up actually became the bandleader. He subsequently wrote many marches and operas. His name was John Phillip Sousa.

Another boy who lived in Sousa's neighborhood but was a little older than us was quite a prankster. His father, Adam George Herold, worked as the chief clerk of the Navy Yard, and the family lived at Eighth Street E, just outside the gates. It was unheard of that people of color of either sex would ever be employed in such a prestigious agency of the government. But the reason I knew of him was because Mother worked cleaning the offices there, and Father and I would wait to take her home in a carriage. There I would see a mischievous boy frolicking about the neighborhood. The father is said to have owned two other adjacent houses, two others elsewhere in the neighborhood, and two other properties in Baltimore. Thinking back, I recall Mr. Withers making reference to the Sousa boy, though he was not his student, and to how prominent a family he came from. In that context he would sometimes talk about their family friends, the Herolds, and how much of a rascal young Davy was. That is when I

[14] Blind Tom's true name was Thomas. He was born blind in Virginia in 1849 to slave parents. It was discovered early that he had a propensity for music, being able to simultaneously play two songs on two different instruments while singing a third.

realized that he was the same boy that Mr. Withers spoke of. In his teen years, before attending Georgetown College, the younger Herold was a pharmacist's deliveryman. I saw him near our old neighborhood once when he delivered medicine to President Buchanan at the White House. His name was David E. Herold. I did not think too much more about him until I was age thirteen and noted that he had managed to achieve some degree of notoriety surrounding certain events that took place in the spring of 1865.

1950s

We lived in an area called Carver Terrace in Northeast Washington at 2005 Maryland Avenue. Specifically we lived in an apartment complex owned by a Stuart Proctor. Up until age eight, we lived in a one-bedroom with a kitchen, dining room, and bathroom. Except for the kitchen and bathroom, the floors were of a wood, parquet design. But the kitchen had a floor of linoleum, a product that had been invented almost exactly a hundred years before. It was here that my curiosity about all things natural and manmade was born, from the curiosity as to who imprinted "Standard" on the toilet and where the waste went to when flushed. Dad could usually answer such inquiries. One answer that he could never adequately explain, however, was to the question as to why people in Australia and the South Pole do not fall off of the earth. He gave every explanation imaginable except the one-word answer: gravity. Just up the hill at the corner of NineteenthStreet was the vantage point at which one was greeted by a panoramic view of Washington, including the cast iron dome of the Capitol, the 555-foot Washington Monument and the neoclassical 1899 Library of Congress. A spectacular display of fireworks could be seen from this point on the Fourth of July. Carver Terrace was not a much better neighborhood than those in which many other blacks lived that Mom urged me to stay away from. This included areas like U Street Northwest, Anacostia, and all of Southwest. Mom had a friend whose son, Robert, became my friend. They lived across the Anacostia River in River Terrace. (Old-timers who remembered the late 1800s still called that river the Eastern Branch.) We'd spend the night with one another, playing soldier and the like. Another friend, Gregory, was in my class, and his mother served as my babysitter until Mom got off work. Dad worked at four o'clock in the afternoon and would pick me up at school to take me there. His working hours sometimes served to my advantage insofar as school discipline was concerned. This was because the teacher was reluctant to detain me after class with the rest of the culprits for fear of making Dad late for work. Gregory and I would play soldier, watch television, and yes, sometimes fight.

Sooner or later Mother would show up to pick me up. We would go home and, though tired, she would fix dinner. This was usually a real treat. Sometimes there would be hamburgers on rolls, pork chops, or steaks. A favorite starchy food was fried potatoes with onions or mashed potatoes with gravy. These staples were usually obtained on Saturday mornings, when Dad and I would go to the Safeway grocery store at Bladensburg Road. Here I would ride in the metal cart while Dad picked up food while I clamored for pies, cookies, and all things sweet. On one such occasion, I put aside the verbal requests and merely seized a stick of candy that was made so that you could whistle through it before eating it. I placed it in my pocket and temporarily forgot about it. Later when Mom was changing my pants, the candy fell out. Well, a whipping ensued that removed any likelihood of future stealing. It was not unlike the old nursery rhyme, "The knave of hearts stole the tarts" and "vowed he'd steal no more." Most kids my age presented a problem to parents who wanted them to eat vegetables. Mom came up with a method to bribe me, so to speak. She would prepare spinach and cut up hard-boiled eggs on it and further encourage me by pointing out that the notoriously strong Popeye regularly ate spinach. This last fact was confirmed by the cartoons that came on Channel 5 after school each day. A quick and tasty snack was Underwood's Deviled Ham in a can, which had been around since 1822.

There were almost all black children at the school but only as a result of neighborhood composition. When I was three years old, the US Supreme Court had required schools to be integrated in the decision Brown v. Board of Education Topeka, Kansas.

At this time Washington was a place of buses, trollies, cars, and lots of traffic. In the summer you could smell the asphalt streets as the hot sun shone upon them. The odor would change when a thunderstorm would hit as the rainwater would create a steam-like effect. During one such storm, Gregory and I witnessed lightning strike and destroy a chimney at a nearby apartment building. Periodically the normal sounds of the city, such as children playing, cars traversing the streets, and horns blowing occasionally, would be interrupted by the loud whine of sirens from police cars, fire engines, or ambulances. The fire trucks came in a wide variety. One ambulance came to the apartment one day as a little girl upstairs had swallowed some Clorox detergent.

Later Dad started working midnights, which eliminated the need for babysitters. It was then that we would fish in the summertime just across from where we'd pick Mom up from her job. She worked at the Naval Weapons Plant, also called the Navy Yard, as a secretary. At 4:30 it seemed as though thousands of employees would stream out, many of whom were black. At this time many black people worked for the federal government in the DC area.

Summers in the 1950s were as interesting as they were hot, both temperature-wise and nationally. Insofar as temperature was concerned, such conversations as the following occurred—conversations that would not have been necessary if air-conditioning was in our world.

Dad said, "It won't be so hot in the church today because it's September and the weather is cooler."

Mom said, "It doesn't matter that the water you're drinking is from the faucet and has not been in the refrigerator because it should be cold now anyway since summer is over."

We would take vacations to places like Brooklyn, New York, in 1956; Detroit, 1957; Atlantic City, 1958; and Philadelphia, 1958. By 1959 I was thought to be mature enough to go to a summer camp four hundred miles away in East Brookfield, Massachusetts, a place I later learned to be the home of baseball great Connie Mack. There I learned sports like boxing, decking Tony from Richmond, Virginia, and son of one of the camp directors. As it turned out, Tony and I became pretty good friends when it was discovered that we were born the same day and on the same year. I also learned baseball and swimming, the former becoming a lifelong passion. Though I was unaware at the time, this was a fairly elite institution, attracting the children of the black middle class for many years. Mom and Dad had first become acquainted with it when they took my godmother there sometime in the 1940s. The first part of the summer was designated for the boys, and the girls came later in the summer. I went back there in 1960 and again in 1966.

On the way back home from Camp Atwater, we stopped in New York City, where I went to the top of the Empire State Building (then the tallest building in the world) and the Statue of Liberty.

During those summers, the car and house were always hot, the latter place relieved only by the aforementioned electric fan. It was no better in Greensboro, where Mom and Dad left me during the summers of 1958 and 1959 with Grandma. My cousins Barbara and Frances and Nona, of whose eye I was obviously the apple, would compete to dote on me. I was treated to Disney movies like the *Shaggy Dog* and *Old Yeller,* albeit at the National Theatre, one of only two in that city that allowed Negroes. No less discriminatory was our requirement to go to the Carnegie Negro Library to obtain books to read. My cousins read books to me like *Noah and His Ark.* [15]

Grandma lived on Gray Street, 1201 to be exact. There was no bathroom per se. There was a toilet on the back porch, placed there as though added as an afterthought. Bathing was done in a tin tub whose water was heated on a woodstove. There was running water into the house from the city waterworks. But it was an overall primitive setup. It often struck my imagination as being what life in Washington was probably like a century ago.

During 1959 there was a shooting somewhere down Gray Street that appeared to be the bloody culmination of an adulterous affair. The name *Luke* stuck in my mind, but I didn't know if he was the paramour or the cuckold. A little girl of the neighborhood, Maxine, appeared to be closely connected to the situation and apparently knew enough that prosecutors sought her testimony. The grownups would throw out bits and pieces of information such as, "Luke shot McAdoo" or "McAdoo was with Luke's wife." In later years I learned from a cousin, who was an adult at the time, that it wasn't McAdoo but Mac Durham and that he was the cuckold. The paramour was a Richard Scott, who was in the habit of having improper relations with Durham's wife, Ama Doris, while he was away on duty as an army paratrooper. As it turns out, the only "Luke" involved was Durham's father-in-law. As children, of course, we were not interested in cluttering up the story with accuracies. Anyhow, this little Maxine was afraid to go in the house because of the blood. My recent information now reveals that it was Maxine's mother who was the

[15] As recently as the time the author began this work, that book has been located among his effects and still bears a due date of July 23, 1958!

"wicked woman" in this story. Scott's body was carried outside with some difficulty inasmuch as he was a very large man. Notwithstanding all of that, Maxine was very comely, and my cousin Dickey and I voiced our desire to "go with" her as we observed her playing outside Grandma's window. Then suddenly, as if ambushed in combat, Grandma rushed in brandishing a switch admonishing us that that kind of talk was "ugly."

Around that same time, a similar killing took place in the rear of Grandmother's house. This time the paramour, Garfield Oliver, was coming from the cuckold's house down the path that we used to play in. He was met by the outraged husband and shot dead on the spot. I never learned of the outcome since I did my independent living for the rest of that summer up in Massachusetts.

1850s

During early 1859, talk was extensive about an adulterous affair coming to a bloody culmination in Lafayette Park across from the White House. The grownups had been gossiping for some time about how a dapper gentleman would come to our neighborhood on Fifteenth Street W. He had apparently rented the house at 383 belonging to Mr. John Gray, a black man, for the purpose of meeting a lady who would come there heavily shawled so as to be disguised. When Mother sent me on errands, I had seen Mr. Gray around his other home on Capitol Hill, where he was a public waiter. Mother and some of the other ladies and men in this mixed black and white neighborhood, however, were too clever to be fooled. Nancy Brown, whose husband Thomas was the White House gardener, once scolded the gentleman for tying Lucifer, his horse, to a tree in violation of a city ordinance. The rumor was that he was the US Attorney for the District of Columbia and also the son of the author of "The Star Spangled Banner." As we later learned, his name was Phillip Barton Key. It reached the point that the ladies in the neighborhood would eagerly gaze out the window almost daily to get a glimpse of this upper-class couple who had come to this working-class neighborhood. Having a particularly good vantage point were the two washerwomen, Mrs. Wise and Mrs. Carter, especially Mrs. Carter, who lived right off the rear alley and who Father sometimes took our laundry to. This alley sometimes served as a means of ingress and egress for the shawled lady. She frequently wore a shawl with twisted silk fringe and bugles and a black bonnet with feathers. When she chose to enter from Fifteenth Street, her actions were no less conspicuous as she was frequently observed by the ladies on that street, among whom were Mrs. M. Lacy of 333 Fifteenth Street, another washerwoman.[16]

Mrs. Bayliss, the mother of one of my school chums, Crittenden Bayliss, would also observe this spectacle. She would sometimes babysit me after school. Crittenden and I would, of course, engage in playing, wrestling, and yes, sometimes fighting. It was on one of these occasions that I got a glimpse of the shawled lady entering the house. I also noticed a string or a ribbon hanging from one of the upstairs shutters.

One teenaged girl, Matilda Seeley, who lived with her parents on L Street N had a bird's-eye view of the alley behind the house at 383 Fifteenth Street as well.[17] The mysterious lady would sometimes use this thoroughfare as a means of ingress to the house in question. Matilda and her mother, not unlike Mrs. Carter and Mrs. Wise, would frequently gaze out that window and could consequently describe to a T the apparel of the lady and man. We children just reveled in the curiosity of their goings and comings. However, to the adults they thought it a much more serious matter. They seemed to think that the woman was Teresa Sickles, the wife of Congressman Dan Sickles of New York. They lived on the west side of Lafayette Square at 14 Jackson Place, just down the block from that place where the slaves were kept in the attic. It appears that at some prearranged signal involving the waving of a handkerchief in the square by Key and the ribbon hanging on the shutter, the two would know to meet at the house to conduct an improper interview. This apparently came after earlier trysts in the Congressional Cemetery on the banks of the Eastern Branch, where it was thought that dead men told no tales. There came a time that a man named Woolridge arranged with Crittenden's mother to take a perch in their upstairs room, where he could have a clear view of the house across the street. I had the impression that he was in some way connected to this Congressman Sickles and sought to confirm the rumors. On Saturday, February 26, 1859, this man was looking out of Crittenden's window from about 10 a.m. until 3 p.m. I never heard that any results came from this vigil. Presumably the shawled lady and dapper gentleman never showed up that day.

This all came to a head on the pleasant Sunday afternoon of February

---

[16] Washington City Directory1858.
[17] Ibid.

27, 1859. Crittenden and I were in the square after church that morning when we saw Key near the edge of the park close to the Sickles's house.

He was ostensibly playing with the Sickles's dog Dandy, who, through apparent familiarity, had come across the street to greet him. While petting Dandy, Key was also slyly waving the handkerchief toward the window in the same motion. Unfortunately for Barton Key, this occurred just as Sickles was confronting his wife, Teresa, insisting that she write out and sign a confession. The contents of that confession later published at Sickles's trial provided details of the affair, including the waving of the handkerchief as a signal. Crittenden and I could not be sure, but we thought we heard a voice coming from the Sickles's house exclaiming something to the effect of, "There's the scoundrel now making signals." Anyway, the next thing we knew Key was headed out of the park in a southeasterly direction, and another man began to engage him in conversation. I don't know if this was part of some contrivance, but it enabled a grim-faced man with a top hat who was rapidly walking toward Key from the north side of the square to catch up with him.

There were a few other passersby in the park, and we all stopped and paid attention when the grim-faced man shouted out, "Key, you scoundrel. You've disgraced my home. Now you must die."[18]

This was obviously Dan Sickles. He then fired a shot at Key, which missed. Key then began to grapple with Sickles, causing him to drop the weapon. But Sickles was a walking arsenal and produced another pistol.[19] As Key screamed, "Murder!" and "Don't murder me," he threw the opera glasses that he used for spotting Teresa in the window at Sickles. This did no good as another shot was fired, hitting Key in the thigh, causing him to fall to the ground, still pleading for his life. The next shot found its mark in Key's chest, pretty much finishing him off. Some men from the clubhouse in the middle of the block carried him from the street inside and laid him on an overturned chair. He died not long afterward I understood. It was a curious thing that the man who had engaged Key in conversation stood against a fence and idly watched the whole bloody transaction. The next few hours saw mobs of people in the streets providing and listening to all manner of

---

[18] Nat Brandt, *The Congressman Who Got Away With Murder* (Syracuse: Syracuse University Press, 1991).
[19] Ibid.

rumor regarding the events. I heard that Sickles was headed up to the home of the attorney general on G Street N to turn himself in. A mob of people followed him there. Much of the same crowd, along with a few additions, again followed him as he made his way back to his house on Lafayette Square to pick up items before going to jail. Here detectives accompanied him into the house. Crittenden and I were able to work our way up to the front of the house and onto the porch. Before being told to quit the porch, I could hear a conversation that sounded like Sickles wanted to go upstairs but that the detectives would allow this only if he promised not to harm his wife. His extreme agitation prompted this concern. But I clearly heard him say to someone, perhaps his wife, "I have killed him."[20] If there is such a thing as poetic justice, perhaps this was it insofar as black Americans are concerned. While we bore no ill will to Key personally, it was mentioned by the adults that perhaps this was retribution for the callous decision issued by Key's uncle, Chief Justice Taney, in that decision involving Dred Scott.

On March 1, 1859, they held Barton Key's funeral at his house at 388 C Street N. It became evident that he must have been well liked as people from all walks of life paid their respects. These included Mrs. M. Payne, a black washerwoman who lived in the alley just across Third Street from Key's house, and a black laborer who was perhaps named after a frontier congressman from Tennessee named David Crockett. Mr. Crockett lived at 324 C Street N, a few doors down from Key. The coffin was in the parlor of the house, which was on the right as one entered the house. Key was dressed in a suit similar to what he would wear to the courthouse, which was behind his house. "He looked very lifelike," accordingly to neighbor Timothy Green, a laborer, who lived around the corner at 220 Third Street W. Someone had placed some roses in his hand.[21]

During the month of March, investigation of the murder began. With Key dead, it was up to President Buchanan to appoint a new US Attorney to try the case. He chose Robert Ould, one of Key's assistants. Ould had been one of our neighbors over near Fifteenth Street. He was now thirty-nine years old, with a thirty-one-year-old wife and four children from an infant to eleven years old. Mrs. Ould's mother lived with them. The rumor in the neighborhood was that he was quite wealthy, worth something like $30,000.

---

[20] Ibid.
[21] Ibid.

However, the papers said that the Key family pressed upon the president to appoint someone to assist. It seemed that the president was less than diligent in doing so, the suggestion being that his connection with the Sickles family affected his sense of justice. The Keys therefore took it upon themselves to hire special prosecutors Charles Johnson and James Carlisle. The latter was a part-time assistant corporation counsel, i.e., city attorney. Ironically, he had once had Sickles as a client for the purpose of negotiating the lease for the house at 14 Jackson Place with Key, who was Sickles's attorney!

One day, Crittenden and I saw the black man named Gray at the house on Fifteenth Street along with Matilla's father, Mr. Seeley. With them were another man and a locksmith. The latter appeared to be breaking into the house. They finally got in. They were so intent on their business at hand that they did not notice my chum and I following them inside. The house had a parlor on the right of the entrance and another parlor and a study area behind it on the left. Upstairs there were two bedrooms with a bed in each. Soiled towels were scattered about, and women's belongings were discovered. We later learned that this search was arranged by one Pendleton, a friend of the Keys, to aid in the prosecution of the case.

During the month of April, Sickles was tried, and my buddy Crittenden was thought to be a crucial witness until local statutes were recalled that would prohibit his testimony. His testimony would have mainly been regarding his observation of the events at the house on Fifteenth Street that actually we both had witnessed. For the same reason, perhaps, they did not call me to the big courthouse on Indiana Avenue. The trial started April 4, 1859, with only fifty seats available for the public. Many people were undaunted by this limitation as many were seen climbing into the windows to get a view of the proceedings. Others stood outside, cursing their inability to enter. Finally in late April, the trial was over. When the verdict was pronounced, there was wild cheering. I learned from the adults that Sickles was acquitted, whatever that meant. Anyway, for the first time in American history, a defense of temporary insanity was used by Sickles, and it worked.

A less-notorious but similar killing took place on the steps of the treasury building the same year. Mary Harris worked at the Treasury Department and had a paramour named Adronious Burroughs, who she killed at the above location. The trial went on through 1859, and Harris was acquitted and promptly married her lawyer.

This marker is at the former site of Walter Reed Army Hospital where a tulip tree once stood and used by Confederate sharpshooters to pick off Union troops inside Fort Stevens.

This view is from the parapet of Fort Stevens today. The authors house is roughly a few yards beyond houses in the foreground. The white structure in the middle distance is roughly the location of the Blair mansions In the close-in Washington suburb of Silver Spring, Maryland.

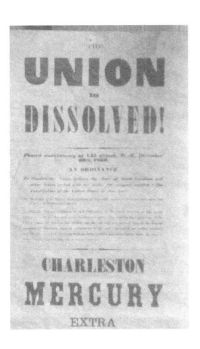

Headline from the South Carolina Mercury
announcing South Carolina's secession

The unfinished monument to George Washington sat near the Potomac
river and the canal. In his fictional childhood, the author describes the
unfinished monument and the foul smell of the canal as the indicator
that the family had arrived back in Washington after a trip to the South.

View of the National Mall today, known as the
"Island," in the nineteenth century

Mason's Island view of Georgetown with Union troops
where the poet Walt Whitman observed training of the First
United States Colored Troops in the summer of 1863

This is the modern day view of Georgetown from Mason's Island, now Roosevelt Island. This where the poet Walt Whitman observed the training of black Union Army troops

This is the present day site of Camp Barker, now occupied by Garrison Elementary School

Former slaves at Camp Barker, some of the forty some
thousand who came to Washington during the Civil War

Montgomery Meigs' Aqueduct Bridge bringing water to Georgetown and
Washington spans Rock Creek. Modern day Rock Creek Parkway runs
under the bridge on the near side of the creek as you view this image.

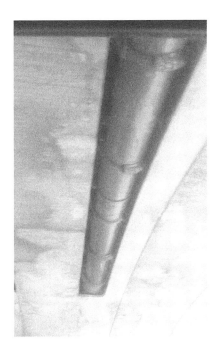

The aqueduct placed by Montgomery Meigs to bring water into Washington in the 1860s is still visible above Rock Creek Parkway

The former site of Murder Bay is now occupied by The Department of Commerce and the District of Columbia City Hall

This is the southeast corner of Lafayette Park
today, the site of Barton Key's murder.

The courthouse that held the trial of Dan Sickles is
now the District of Columbia Court of Appeals.
The office of James Carlisle, Assistant Corporation Counsel, and
hired as special prosecutor by the Key family, occupied the same
office and in the same capacity as the author in his actual adult life.

This is the place on the "Island" where Dr. Lowe launched
his reconnaissance balloon in June of 1861. Ironically it
was roughly where the National Air and Space Museum is
currently located, just out of the picture to the right.

Site of Dr. Lowe's balloon launch with the City Canal
flowing in front of the unfinished capitol

The National Archives now occupies the spot of the Center Market which backed to the old canal. The cars in the picture are on Constitution Avenue under which the old canal still flows.

When the author as a nineteenth century boy would see these locomotives in the Maryland Avenue rail yard, he and the other citizens would be alerted to Rebel activity in nearby Virginia. Ironically, the author spent the first eight years of his actual life living on another part of Maryland Avenue.

The Old Capitol Prison sat where the U.S. Supreme Court now sits just east of the capitol building. This is how it looked when Mary Surratt, Rose Greenhow and Dr. Samuel Mudd were at various times involuntary guests there.

1950s

In 1955 the grownups were talking about how a black lady down in Montgomery, Ms. Parks, would not give up her seat on a bus to a white person, citing tiredness from working. There was also a boy from Chicago who was visiting his grandfather down in Mississippi and supposedly whistled at a white woman in 1954. He was promptly seized from the house and beaten mercilessly and then shot for good measure. Needless to say, this resulted in his death. His mother insisted that when he was funeralized in Chicago that his coffin remain open to display to the world the savagery that raged in the hearts of Southerners when it came to people of color. Shortly after the murder, two suspects were identified and brought to trial. True to the pattern displayed in most Southern trials involving white defendants and black victims during this era, the accused were acquitted because of "lack of evidence." Ironically, the first year in which there was no recorded lynching of a black person in America since the 1880s was the year of my birth, 1951.

I started first grade in September 1957 at Charles Young elementary school, which was named for a black World War I hero. My starting school was fairly routine, unlike the plight of many of my fellow black school children who attempted to matriculate into Central High School in Little Rock that same month. At my school, my dear teacher, Mrs. Flipping, was in the doorway to tenderly guide us to the right classroom. Imagine the plight of those students in Little Rock and elsewhere when, instead of a benevolent teacher tenderly greeting them, Governor Orville Faubus was standing in the doorway to "tenderly" deny them ingress by threatening them with bodily harm for no other reason than to deprive them of a quality education. Quite a contrast. The grownups said President Eisenhower had to make him let them in by use of the National Guard.

Around 1958 I was made to take piano lessons from a Mr. Jones, an elderly gentleman who would come to the house. Through him I learned such complex musical arrangements as "The Funny Little Bunny" and "I Would Like an Ice Cream Cone." The idea of learning to play the piano was not totally adverse to me. My only problem was that practice time frequently cut out my time to play baseball and the like with the boys who I could see out the window. These lessons went on for a few more years and included other teachers. By 1959 I had advanced to a proficiency of unimaginable levels. I was now playing such tunes as "Myrtle the Turtle" and "The Eskimo" with both hands on the piano! Mom used as an example of what I could accomplish if I only applied myself like little Stevie Wonder, a child prodigy born the year before I was. Somehow, even at age eight I perceived that one would have to be blind to achieve such proficiency. No thanks.[22]

In late 1959 and the early 1960s, I was involved in the Cub Scouts and later the Boy Scouts. We would take many excursions and take part in many local activities, including picnics and all sorts of activities. Dad was irate when I struck out "looking" in a softball game sponsored by the Scouts. He gruffly told me, "We have work on your hitting."

An interesting trip involved a trip to a fire station that Dad encouraged because it would provide that answer to a question that I pestered him with frequently. The question was how the fire department knew the location of a fire. The fire station trip revealed that an intricate electric system tracing the source of a call was the answer. Additionally, large trucks with immense pumping capacity were connected to water main outlets called hydrants that were placed throughout the city that enabled them to effectively control most fires. There were smaller ones that had ladders and hoses on the side and a larger hook and ladder that would enable firemen to reach the upper levels of buildings and cause a substantial stream of water to douse a fire. How haphazard the operation must have been in years past when horse-drawn wagons were used and pumpers were connected to wooden hydrants. Other excursions included trips to museums, such as the wax museum located in the Foggy Bottom neighborhood. The various wax figures seemed almost lifelike as they depicted various scenes

---

[22] Stevie Wonder's true name was Steveland Morris. He was born blind in 1950 in Saginaw, Michigan. His abilities include composition and proficiency on the harmonica and the piano.

in American history. Particularly haunting was an image of Captain John Smith about to be executed by the Powhatans, in which the curators of the museum had actually managed to cause him to breathe in and out. The scene showed the princess Pocahontas imploring her father, the chief, to spare the Englishman. While there we saw a stately old lady walking with escorts. Her dress was reminiscent of what my grandmother seemed to wear, and she had a parasol protecting her from the sun. One of the adults accompanying us whispered that she thought it was Alice Longworth, the daughter of President Theodore Roosevelt. Ironically, the location where we saw her was within view of the island in the Potomac named after her famous father.[23]

The scout troop that I initially belonged to was headquartered at our church and was located in a fairly rough neighborhood. Consequently, the fellow scouts were of a different background than myself, a fact that was never lost on Mom as she constantly informed me that I was of a better background than they were. This was probably not unlike the class distinction that existed in this city when former slaves descended on Washington in the 1860s, much to the dismay of the free and fairly well-off blacks that were already here. I can imagine a young boy a hundred years ago having his mother tell him the same thing about the many former slaves who lived in Murder Bay or Nigger Hill.

---

[23] Theodore Roosevelt was the youngest man to become president by virtue of his succession to the office when President William McKinley was assassinated on September 6, 1901. McKinley died on September 14, and Roosevelt took office that day at age forty-two.

1850s

There was one white man that Mother and Father thought was of the right attitude about colored folk. That was a man named John Brown. This man decided that the only way the sins of this country would be purged was with blood. By taking the federal arsenal at Harper's Ferry, Virginia, John Brown would arm slaves in the immediate vicinity and then arm other slaves, eventually freeing all the slaves in the South. One Sunday night in October, Brown, two of his sons, and some former slaves all struck, seizing the arsenal temporarily. Father said the militia came and there was a shootout, resulting in the deaths of his sons and his wounding. The militia was led by the owner of that house across the river that we could see with the spyglass with the tall oak trees guarding the entrance. He stood trial in Charlestown and pleaded his own case from a stretcher. He was found guilty and ultimately was sentenced to hang on December 2, 1859. They say he took one last look at the beautiful Blue Ridge Mountains and said something to the effect that this was a beautiful land. Then he proudly mounted the scaffold to engage in the dance of death, kissing a black woman's baby on the way up. Father and Mother both figured that his statement about purging by blood was a prediction of some bloody conflict about to brew. In the crowd were two people whose names I heard again a few years later. These two were members of the Virginia militia who were sent to Charlestown pursuant to rumors that a posse was en route to that place to accomplish a dramatic last-minute rescue of old John Brown from the gallows. One was John McCausland, who came to my fair city in 1864 very much without welcome as a Confederate general. The other was a fledgling actor who had joined the Virginia militia for no other purpose than to thwart any attempt to rescue Brown. However, I understood that he was quickly convinced that military life to include death and killing were not for him. It appears that as Brown made the final plunge and engaged in the dance of death, this man vomited uncontrollably and was thereby convinced that he would best serve society as a thespian. His name was John Wilkes Booth. Father and Mother mentioned him frequently thereafter. Apparently he received rave reviews for his Shakespearean performances at the likes of Grover's National Theatre and Ford's Theatre in Washington and other theatres in Baltimore, Philadelphia, and New York. But they were never remiss in reminding me that he was no friend to our race.

1960S

During the summer of 1960, I went back to that camp in Massachusetts. This time I learned the game of baseball to the point that I could always draw a walk. I couldn't hit, mind you, but I knew the strike zone extremely well. I would sometimes call home and ask what was on television. Mom would say that nothing was on but the conventions. I later learned that this is when the Vice President Nixon was seeking the Republican nomination for president.

I really became a "man" that summer at the ripe old age of eight. My biggest nightmare came to pass, and I survived it. This was to become ill while far away from home and from Mom's tender care. I endured this man-like, reporting myself to the infirmary and joining another camper there. We recuperated listening to the Boston Red Sox games on the radio. When the camp season was over, we came back to Washington, stopping in New York and Philadelphia to see relatives. When I got home, I could see that a young senator from Massachusetts was seeking to run against Nixon for the Democrats. The big event of that summer for us was the preparation to move to a new neighborhood and a house. From Carver Terrace we would move to an area near the city limits that had reached prominence during the Civil War. This was called Brightwood, whose principal thoroughfare was Georgia Avenue. I began the school year at Charles Young, but three weeks later I had to transfer to Brightwood Elementary School. Moving day was September 20, 1960. This house had three bathrooms, three bedrooms, a basement, and an attic. What stood out to me on that first day of school was the large chairs for the students. Even more, for the first time I saw that I would be attending school with white children. This phenomenon was given further background by Mrs. Saffrit, the teacher. She explained how the old red building visible out the classroom window and just across Missouri Avenue had been established for the colored children shortly after the Civil War. The building we could see was actually built in 1912 replacing an old wooden structure that had been built from timbers recovered from the dismantling of nearby Fort Stevens at the end of the war. It served the purpose of colored education until about the time I was born, when the national trend was toward the integration of public schools. Thus, my present attendance at Brightwood was the product of a radical and recent change from what had been a longstanding tradition of segregation. While there, I became a safety patrol boy under a system where we were assigned to squads that were based on the geography surrounding the school. I was assigned to the school squad on Nicholson Street, where the school was located. My buddies were on the Georgia squad named after the nearby avenue, and the Madison squad, after the next street over from the school. I had once considered joining a buddy on the latter squad until I got an eerie feeling every time I went over there, so I changed my mind. There was one particular house that looked out of place among the neighboring houses on that street. They said something about an old Swissman who had lived there in the nineteenth century who had put in one of the first indoor bathrooms in the outlying area of Washington during that time. It appears that when the nineteenth century left, he didn't.

During that autumn, much attention was paid to the presidential race. The young senator referred to before was John F. Kennedy. He was a Catholic, and if elected, he would be the first president of that religion. He would also be the youngest man to be elected president at the age of forty-three. Mom and Dad thought he was a good man who would do right by black Americans. They were not too sure about his opponent, Vice President Richard M. Nixon. At church and other social gatherings of black people, the talk was of the expected good that Kennedy would do for our race. On November 8, 1960, Kennedy was elected the thirty-fifth president of the United States in one of the closest elections of all time. So throughout the Christmas season, there was a new president-elect. It snowed on December 18, 1960, but was clear by Christmas Day. An intervening event between these two dates was Mom and Dad's sixteenth wedding anniversary. For Christmas I got a battleship called the *Fighting*

Lady and an airplane called the *Flying Fox.* These came from either Santa Claus or Children's Supermarket.

On January 19, 1961, a tremendous snowstorm hit Washington. On occasions such as this, schools were frequently closed and the children would enjoy an unscheduled vacation. But this time it was somewhat of a raw deal because schools were closed anyway because this man Kennedy was to be inaugurated that day. Once again I watched on television as a man made a speech in the cold, but this time Dad was here, unlike 1953. Kennedy had such charisma that his speech was quoted and memorized by many. His appeal was not unlike that which I had read about the president who had been elected exactly one hundred years before him, Abraham Lincoln. Phrases like, "And so my fellow Americans, ask not what your country can do for you, but what you can do for your country" became popular. At age nine, his presence was such that I actually paid attention to the substance of his speech. He made reference to sending a man to the moon and returning him back safely to earth again. While his vision was ambitious to be sure, he warned, "All this will not be finished in the first hundred days or even in the first thousand days, nor in the lifetime of this administration or in our own lifetime on this planet, but let us begin." He also said, "Whether you are citizens of America or citizens of the world, ask not what America can do for you, but what together we can do for the freedom of man. And finally, whether you are citizens of America or citizens of the world, ask of us the same high standards of strength and sacrifice that we ask of you. With a good conscience our only sure reward, with history the final judge of our deeds, let us go forth and lead the land we love, asking His blessing and His help but knowing that here on earth, God's work must truly be our own."

Yes, 1961 came in full of promise of prosperity. In our new neighborhood, we were only one of a few black families living there. It appeared now that Mom and Dad were actually middle class Americans. School was challenging and interesting. I prided myself on new information learned and frequently recited it at dinner. A new passion also came over me: baseball. I ate, slept, and drank it. The Senators played that year at Griffith Stadium, where we had gone in the '50s. But now there was a new team, ironically still called the Senators. The original Senators who had played (term used loosely) in Washington since 1859 under the name

Nationals and came to the American League in 1901 had become part of a trend in which owners moved teams to ostensibly greener pastures. Those pastures in this case were in the Upper Midwest, Minneapolis to be exact. Yes, the Senators had become the Minnesota Twins. But that same year, baseball decided to add two new teams to the American League, the Los Angeles Angels and the new Washington Senators. I followed every game on radio or television, cried when they lost, and exalted when they won. (The crying exceeded the exultation by far.) Once the team had a promotion in which some food product would be donated to orphaned children whenever a Senator hit a homerun. Dad enjoyed commenting that if those poor children were waiting on the Senators to hit a homerun they would surely "perish to death." In fact, the 1961 Washington Senators had the worst record in the history of baseball. But we only retained that title for a year because in 1962 when the National League expanded, bringing in the Houston Colt 45s and the New York Mets, the latter team promptly acquired that honor.

Yes baseball was such a passion for me that Dad would frequently ask, "Boy, can we talk about something other than baseball?"

My fourth-grade teacher, Mrs. Safrit, commented on our news report assignments that my articles were good but that they should be about something other than baseball. She also told Mom that if I could play the sport as well as I talked it, I would make a lot of money one day. Mom asked me to start being interested in something other than baseball. I complied, just as soon as football season started.

Overall, Mr. Kennedy was a very popular president. Obviously it was rare to see him in person because of all of the protection. However, I did see him once from a distance. That was on July 10, 1962, at about three hundred feet away. The occasion was the All-Star baseball game at the new DC Stadium. Dad managed to get tickets in the left field upper deck, the president being directly across the field behind the first-base dugout. We saw him throw out the ceremonial first pitch. I recall looking down on a halo most of that game. In those days the Los Angeles Angels had halos on the top of their caps. The one I saw belonged to the American League left fielder Leon Wagner. That was a classic combination of players with the great Mickey Mantle and Roger Maris in the outfield along with

Wagner. For the National League, the greater Hank Aaron, Willie Mays, and Roberto Clemente were in their outfield.

On the international front, the new president had to deal with the issue of a Communist regime just ninety miles from American shores in Cuba. The possibility of war with Russia and/or Cuba was not too far-fetched. One April day the teacher talked about how the United States broke diplomatic relations with Cuba. That same month, President Kennedy ordered a secret mission in which he trained Cuban refugees to launch an attack on Cuba to remove the dictator Fidel Castro from power. The place of the attack was at el Bahia de Conchos, the Bay of Pigs. This proved a huge failure and the first negative mark in the new president's administration. Still, a full-scale Cold War was in place between the United States and Russia, along with Cuba, over communism. Perhaps it can be said that the first shots of that war were that April day in 1961. On April 12, 1961, a war of sorts began as Russia and the United States competed in the space race. On this day, the Russian Cosmonaut Yuri Gagarin became the first human in space, winning the first battle of that war.

I was now firmly entrenched in school and enjoying it. I learned all about the early exploration of the Americas by the Europeans. Glorified in these events were the likes of Fernando Magellan, Vasco da Gama, and Christopher Columbus. Their deeds certainly seemed on the surface worthy enough for glorification; however, little information seemed to be given to the plight of the indigenous people whom they encountered in the Americas. While Cortes and Pizarro were touted as the conquerors of Mexico and Peru, respectively, the teacher never emphasized the terrible destruction of two wonderful civilizations of the Aztecs and Incas, respectively.

Overall, however, life was good in what was characterized as a middle-class existence. I would generally walk the three or four blocks to school with other kids in the neighborhood. Directly en route were the remains of an old fort that had been prominent in the Civil War. According to a plaque, it had originally been called Fort Massachusetts and later renamed Fort Stevens. It had high earthworks and cannon ports with a deep trench around it. There was a rock sitting on the parapet with a depiction of some portion of the battle that took place there. In this illustration, a man is getting shot just a few feet away from another man with a tall stovetop hat. The man with the hat it was said was President Abraham Lincoln, who had come to watch the battle. From that vantage point he could have looked directly into what was now our living room window. The kids and I rarely wasted an opportunity to play there. In the spring of 1963, the teacher talked of a tragedy in the Atlantic involving a submarine called the *Thresher*. This type of ship had been in its infancy during the Civil War when almost exactly a hundred years before a ship called the *Hunley* repeatedly sank with men aboard until it was perfected. Now apparently notwithstanding a hundred years of development, the submarine *Thresher* ended up like its predecessor, disabled at the bottom of the North Atlantic. Unlike the *Hundley*, it was never raised. It was thought that the men died from an implosion according to the teacher (i.e., the water pressure at the floor of the ocean crushed it).

During this time, the city's recreation department had established playground football and baseball leagues. I played both sports for the Fort Stevens playground, which was named after that battery that could still be seen in the neighborhood from the Civil War. I had a particularly good football game against the boys from Emery playground. The field was located on a particularly imposing point of land that overlooked the city. I mused about how a house there would serve as a strategic military purpose as it was close to several remaining Civil War forts like Slocum, DeRussey, Totten, and now Stevens. Maybe a prominent person did have a home there in the last century.

Dad was still with the special police and guarded the Joint Chiefs of Staff at the Pentagon. Mom had left the Navy Department and was now beginning a new career as a teacher. She achieved this objective by attending District of Columbia Teacher's College at night. This institution had been founded in 1851 by a white woman from New York named Myrtilla Miner as the Colored Girls School. Its original focus was the training of black women as primary school teachers and in domestic skills. Until about the time I was four years old, it was known as Miner Teacher's College. We continued to go on vacations to the likes of Atlantic City, Detroit, Canada, Philadelphia, and New York. Interspersed with these trips were visits to the relatives in North Carolina. My maternal grandparents were now deceased, but both paternal grandparents and several aunts, uncles, and cousins still lived there in North Carolina. Baseball still being a passion, I played continuously on the farmland with the young cousins. Immediately prior to one trip, Dad and I had been watching the Senators play the Tigers on television from Detroit. During that game, the Tigers' first baseman, Norm Cash, hit a homerun that cleared the right field roof of Tiger Stadium and landed on Michigan Avenue. When we got to Granddad's farm at Siler City in June of 1961, I immediately envisioned the old barn with its two-storied hayloft and roof, situated what seemed like miles from the house, as my own little Tiger Stadium. I immediately set about the task of tossing up a ball and hitting it over that roof. After several attempts, I was able to rush into the house and truthfully announce that I had cleared the roof of the barn (a.k.a., Tiger Stadium).

1860s

With the bloody end to John Brown's attempt to free the slaves at that place in Virginia, some species of ferry, Father and Mother seemed to think somehow a new beginning was at hand. They displayed an inexplicable sense of optimism for our people. I didn't quite understand that because from what everything I understood the old man was defeated in that shootout in the arsenal. In fact, two black men and two of the old man's sons were killed. How could there be optimism?

Well now I was back in school at the Negro academy. Ironically I had thought that I would be under the instruction of S. J. Thompson, the teacher at the male grammar school at W Fourteenth Street and Q Street N. That did not take place because of my color. It was a constant source of irritation to Father that blacks had to pay taxes to support city schools but their children were not allowed to go. Some fellow developed a new type of floor in 1860 called linoleum. We were about to have some put down in the house on Fifteenth Street, but it never occurred since in September 1860 we left Fifteenth Street and moved to the outlying community of Brightwood. This area was some five miles north of the capital city and was largely farmland. About thirty-one families were living in this community, of which five were black, including us. Our family was the only black household not headed by a women, and we all lived largely in Vinegar Hill. Six of the white families owned slaves, but four of those families owned only one slave. Among the community's denizens was Mathew Gault Emery, a former mayor of Washington. His house sat upon a high bluff overlooking Seventh Street Road. Emory Methodist Church was on that same street and across from Mr. Emory's house. One nice lady was a dairywoman named Betty Thomas who lived near the church. Father said the community was originally called Brighton because of the post office established by Mr. Lewis Burnett at the corner of Milkhouse Road and the Seventh Street Road. The name was later changed to Brightwood because mail had become confused because of a community called Brighton in Montgomery County, Maryland.

Life was different now because of the relative quiet of the area outside the city. The playmates I acquired now were largely white. The Locust Farm was just off of the Seventh Street Road. At one point the owner placed an ad in the *Washington Star* for a sober farmhand. Father considered applying, but it would have meant leaving us to live there. There was a church very near called Emory Methodist Church. It would have been so much more convenient to go there than all the way downtown. But because of our color, we could not go.

I began to play the New York game. I became good enough to be effective as the striker. Now I took a greater interest when Father would take me to see the Nationals play. Our connection with the city was primarily the Seventh Street Road. The entire federal district known as Columbia had increased its population significantly in the past few years, largely because of foreign immigration. There were many Irishmen, Germans, and Dutchmen now calling Washington City and its surrounding areas their homes. This contributed to an 1860 population of 75,080, of which 60, 764 were white, 11, 131 free blacks, and 3,185 slaves.

While that first autumn was a fairly happy one personally, it was not so much nationally. It seemed that the acts of that old man in Virginia last year had polarized the country between North and South. They say that the members of Congress had a clear division on issues depending whether they represented Northern or Southern states. Even within these divisions there were other partisan divisions. The Democrats had convened in Charleston in April. But the issue of slavery caused a split with the Northern Democrats led by Stephen A. Douglas of Illinois and the Southerners by John Bell of Tennessee. They later convened again up the road in Baltimore but could not reach accord. The result was the nomination of three Democrats, Douglas, John C. Breckenridge, and Bell, to run against the Republican Abraham Lincoln. Though also divided, the Republicans nominated Lincoln as a moderate on the issue of slavery. He and his running mate, Hannibal Hamlin of Maine, felt that the Constitution protected slavery where it existed but that it was not to be spread to the territories. On November 6, 1860, Abraham Lincoln was elected in one of the closest elections of all time based on popular votes. He had 1,866,452, roughly 39 percent, with Douglas a close second with 1, 376,957. Had the voters cast their ballot for him instead of the other two candidates, Bell and Breckinridge, Lincoln would have been defeated. We black folks figured he was really an abolitionist but did not want to be too vocal about it. I understood that that was someone who did not like slavery. Too bad Mother and Father couldn't vote. On December 5, the first snow fell. It snowed again on December 18, making things Christmassy. I used to hear people talking about how not too long ago, Christmas was not the festive occasion that it is now. It was only as late as the early 1830s that the first state, Louisiana, made it a holiday. Ironically, it had been an occasion to celebrate with food, drink, and dance in Europe centuries ago. However, it was the Puritans from England who subdued the celebration when they came to America. They marked the occasion by somberness and reflection upon one's sins, both past and future. This attitude persisted until roughly thirty years ago. Throughout this now happy time of year, great apprehension consumed the country. At school and church, in every conversation you heard the fear was that a great war between North and South was imminent. Before Lincoln was elected, South Carolina had threatened to withdraw from the United States if he won. Five days before Christmas, Mother and Father's anniversary, what appeared to be the realization of that old man's prediction and South Carolina's threat came to pass. The *Washington Star* was emblazoned with a headline saying the "Union Is Dissolved." Needless to say, Christmas was not the joyous occasion it normally was. However, for us black folks it was not necessarily believed that a war would be a bad thing. Father said maybe slavery would meet its demise through a great conflict. Notwithstanding the national crises, I did receive from St. Nick or Stuntz's Toy Store at 1207 New York Avenue some hand-carved soldiers and some oranges. Needless to say, Stuntz's was one of my favorite places to go with its awninged windows and painted sign out front. Although we became familiar with the concept of this St. Nick from a poem written about forty years before by a man from New York named Clement Clark Moore, it was hard to picture that character—that is, until Thomas Nast placed an illustration in the newspaper. That made the character very real for us children. The typical gifts from this jolly old fellow were hand-carved toys, cakes, oranges, and apples. Moore had described him in his poem "A Visit from St. Nicholas," but Nast's depiction was much more vivid.

On March 4, 1861, Lincoln made a speech down in front of the Capitol. A large barricade was placed between him and the crowd as apparently there had been threats made that he would not live until his inauguration. He obviously made it that far. Indeed, once he finished the speech, his route down Pennsylvania Avenue en route back to the White House was lined with soldiers with fixed bayonets at the direction of the secretary of war, Cameron. The carriage in which he and the outgoing President Buchanan rode was surrounded by cavalry. In his speech, Lincoln said things that even a nine-year-old found fascinating enough to remember. This was largely because what he said seemed to make it all the more puzzling that Mother and Father would find him to be such a friend to the black race. In his speech on March 4, he quoted from another speech that he had given in which he said, "I have no purpose, directly or indirectly to, interfere with the institution of slavery in the states where it exists. I believe I have no lawful right to do so, and I have no inclination to do so." Many of the black folks still saw this as a reason for optimism inasmuch as the man clearly had no intention of allowing slavery to be further spread. But he also seemed to give full support to that law that Mother had warned me about where some white man could swear that we were his slaves and the matter would be concluded.

About this Lincoln said, "There is much controversy about the delivering up of fugitives from service or labor. The clause I now read is as plainly written in the Constitution as any other of its provisions: 'No person held to service or labor in one state, under the laws thereof, escaping into another, shall, in consequence of any law or regulation therein, be discharged from such service or labor, but shall be delivered up on claim of the party to whom such service or labor may be due.'"

Nevertheless, the general feeling about Lincoln among black folk was that deep inside he hated slavery and was not necessarily an enemy to us. Yes, upon his inauguration there was cause for optimism. By the time of his speech, Father said some other states had joined South Carolina in seceding from the United States. In fact, some guy made a similar speech exactly a month earlier in Montgomery, Alabama. His name was Davis, and he was the president of his "country." His vice president also spoke. The newspaper quoted part of his speech that said something to the effect that his country was founded on the great truth of the white race's superiority to the black race. Mother and Father were in no way disillusioned in thinking that these fellows were friends to the black race.

The first shots of the anticipated and dreaded war occurred at 4:30 on the morning of April 12, 1861. It appeared that the Southerners demanded that the garrison stationed at Fort Sumter in Charleston abandon the fort and remove Old Glory while they were at it. The gallant Colonel Robert Anderson declined and resisted the bombardment. Two days later the Southerners' bombardment proved too formidable, and the garrison was obliged to surrender the fort. The Southerners had obviously won the first battle of the war. We now heard in Washington that President Lincoln called for seventy-five thousand volunteers for three months to put down the rebellion. In response to this, thousands of soldiers packed our city, coming from all quarters. One of the regiments that came was the Sixth Massachusetts from the town of Oxford in that state. Their journey, however, was apparently not uneventful. I personally encountered many of them while passing by that infirmary on Judiciary Square. They were being treated for broken bones and bruises incurred as they attempted to walk from Camden Station to President's Station in the city of Baltimore. Evidently a crowd of Southern sympathizers in that city attacked them and started a veritable riot as they attempted to reach Washington. Ironically, there was a woman working as a clerk at the Patent Office who was from the same hometown as many of these soldiers. She was conspicuous as she was frequently seen moving about among the soldiers in the infirmary and the Senate chamber of the Capitol building treating the wounded and sick on her own accord. She would even bring pots and pans and food from her apartment at Seventh Street W less than a block from the post office that Father and I used to go to, to help provide for the soldiers. After soliciting charitable items from Massachusetts for the benefit of their native sons, this one-room apartment became overburdened. She, therefore, arranged for the items to be stored by an army quartermaster. One time on a visit to the Capitol with Father, we heard her reading aloud from the rostrum the newspaper of her hometown to the soldiers. I saw her many times before learning her name. She was about five feet tall, with an expressive face. Not particularly comely, she walked with an air of resolution and strength. She obviously made an impact with tireless efforts at the beginning of this great conflict, but it was much later that some of her subsequent achievements enabled me to learn that her name was Clara Barton.

The Massachusetts men and for that matter white men were not the only ones who responded to the call of duty for the country. Father and several other black men of the city responded. I was at once proud and afraid for Father. However, the resolve displayed by him and Jacob Dobson were quite noteworthy. The latter implored Secretary of War Simon Cameron to use black men by way of the following correspondence on April 23, 1861:

> Sir: I desire to inform you that I have some three hundred reliable colored free citizens of this City, who desire to enter the service for the defense of the City. I have been three times across the Rocky Mountains in the service of the country with Fremont and others. I can be found about the Senate Chambers, as I have been employed about the premises for some years.

Indeed, Dodson was not a man whose offer should have been taken lightly, for he had, at eighteen years of age in 1843, then a free young black man of Washington, indeed displayed extraordinary prowess as an adventurer with Fremont and performed manfully. He shared many adventures and hardships along the Oregon Trail and had always displayed courage and fidelity.

On June 18, 1861, Dr. Thaddeus Lowe startled the citizens of the city by causing some species of balloon called the *Enterprise* to float over the city. Some months prior to its launching, an impressive staging area had been set up near the launch site. Against a backdrop of old brick houses with slanted tin roofs and multiple chimneys and the spiraling brick smokestack of the newly created Washington Gas Company along Maryland and Missouri Avenues, Dr. Lowe had set up light-colored gas-generating wagons. One could see the deflated *Enterprise* awaiting its flight preparation against the larger backdrop of the partially completed dome of the US Capitol, all situated in a neighborhood notorious for crime and danger. On that June day, it was launched from the Island at about Seventh Street W and B Street South. This was such a tremendous feat that I would imagine there being some future structure being placed there to commemorate the accomplishment. The balloon soared to about five hundred feet and was towed by some species of rope to a point where President Lincoln could view it. A few of us standing near the White House could see him as he viewed it from an upstairs window. To put the final exclamation point on the occasion, Dr. Lowe transmitted the first air-to-ground message to the president by way of a telegraph line to the ground saying, "Dear sir: This point of observation commands an area nearly fifty miles in diameter. The city, with its girdle of encampments, presents a superb scene. I have pleasure in sending you this first dispatch ever telegraphed from an aerial station." To add just an additional bit of flair, a bugler went up and gave a rendition of "Taps."

Sometimes we would spy similar contraptions over the city, and Mother would playfully say, "One day I'm going to put you in one of them."

The concept of this aerial observation took hold in the great conflict about to occur. By use of balloons, Union troops were able to ascertain troop movement by the enemy and thus be able to better counterattack the Rebels. In fact, Dr. Lowe's very contraption was the target of Rebel sharpshooters in its reconnaissance mission but was apparently too high for any mischief to take place. Not to be outdone, however, the Rebels came up with an underwater method of attacking our navy vessels. Some species of vessel was developed that could go underwater with men inside. I understood that in the experimental stage of this tactic, some men aboard a ship called the *Hunley* met with horrible fates as the vessel failed to come to the surface on a few occasions. They apparently suffocated or the vessel imploded from water pressure, as evidenced by the attitudes on their faces when it was brought to the surface. It was eventually perfected and did some little damage to some of our ships, including the *Cumberland* and the *Congress*.

Father and the aforementioned Mr. Dodson were inspired by that famous man that I could never get a good look at during church, Mr. Douglass. He reportedly said, "When the first shells shattered the walls of Sumter, I predicted then and there that the war would not be fought entirely out by white men." He also said, "Who would be free must themselves strike the blow," and "Freedom won by white men loses half its luster." He, unlike most Americans, had not lost sight of the fact that black men from Maryland and Virginia had fought during the Revolution and that black sailors during the War of 1812 had dragged cannons from the Navy Yard under the command of Commodore Joshua Barney for use in the battle of Bladensburg Heights. However, the resolve of the instant would-be volunteers was rivaled only by the War Department's hasty resolve not to include them in the war. Rejection of their services was swift. Secretary of War Cameron replied to Mr. Dobson as follows:

"In reply to your letter of the twenty-third instant, I have to say that this Department has no intention at present to call into service of Government any colored soldiers."[24]

Thus rejected, black men had to temporarily wait in the wings while white men fought to uphold the Constitution. The wave of patriotism was intense among both white and black people. Despite the rejection, black men were undaunted in their efforts to, at once, show their patriotism and their manliness. Indeed they would form their own regiments and drill in the streets until they were warned by police that they could not protect them from the increasing resentment of the white populous.

By 1863 the president authorized the enlistment of black troops by way of the Emancipation Proclamation. However, that did nothing to curtail resentment bordering on violence whenever the men attempted to drill. The first regiment thus formed by the newly created Bureau of Colored Troops, aptly named the First US Colored Infantry, was formed in Washington City. One company, B, had some twelve of their eighty-two men natives of Washington City. This regiment's response to the white hostility was to leave the city under cover of darkness and set up camp on Mason's Island in the Potomac. For a citizen to access their location, the most direct route was to venture up Pennsylvania Avenue into Georgetown by way of the aqueduct bridge, the same one that Meigs brought water to the city through and onto a rocky road to the Island. I took that route on July 11, 1863, with Crittenden to gaze upon veritable heroes of our race. While there, we saw a gray-haired and gray-bearded man sitting on a rock near the water, apparently recording events as they

---

[24] Letter from Secretary of War Simon Cameron summarily rejecting the collective offers of all would-be black volunteers.

occurred. This was near a white stucco house with several shade trees. It is said that the house had belonged to Virginia Mason, the author of the infernal Fugitive Slave Act. From that place, the white-haired man could spy the camp of the First USCT consisting of neat white tents. Some were bathing in the river and washing their clothes. It appeared that on that hot day, the locust, sassafras, and spice trees made it tolerable. Distant sounds of the city were discernable from here, and the puffing of steamers up and down the river were seen. From this vantage point, the Capitol could be seen some three or four miles away through a pleasant blue of a July haze. Grapevines and trumpet flowers adorned this spot as birds sang cheerfully. That in combination with the fragrance and freshness in the air made this an overall pleasant spot. We later saw the white-haired man on a rock near the yellowish, muddy water, a product of recent rains upriver. Near him was wildlife such as water snakes, and the scene was surrounded by verdant hills on the heights surrounding the river. Now the soldiers were about to be paid; it appeared to be about a thousand men. A white man in an army uniform with a gold leaf on his color (Father says that means he is a major) sat at a table with papers and a box of money before him. Names were called, and black men walked up and were remunerated for their services. Several men were named George Washington, Daniel Webster, Horace Greely, Alfred Tennyson, John Brown, and John Quincy Adams. The first group we saw got paid $10.03 per man, presumably for a month's service. Then another company got $5.36 per man. Then we heard some little cursing and complaining when Cos. K and I received twenty-three and seventy cents per man, respectively. After a few received this pay, most marched off to their quarters unpaid rather than to accept this paltry sum. I understand that this was an ongoing problem for black men throughout this conflict and that there were many on all fronts who refused pay until it corresponded with that of white soldiers as they had been promised.[25] The white-haired man was Walt Whitman, we learned.

Washington's physical appearance, though generally the same as in the fifties, had taken on a new persona with the war. For example, in October of 1862, one traveling about the city would note that it was surrounded by hills and three bridges over the Potomac. These were the Long Bridge,

---

[25] Walter Lowenfelds, *Walt Whitman's Civil War* (New York, New York: Da Capo Press, 1960).

the Aqueduct Bridge from Georgetown over Rock Creek, and the Chain Bridge, which spanned the river further north. The aforementioned Long Bridge was accessed from the city by the prominent Maryland Avenue. That thoroughfare took on a specific significance because of the rail yard immediately before the Long Bridge. As the war progressed, that portion of the avenue came to be a gauge as to the proximity of General Lee's army by noting the number of locomotives on the tracks, a large number signifying that the Confederates were nearby and the trains had been brought within the safe confines of the city to preclude capture. Speaking of the aforementioned general, one could still see that mansion on the hills that he owned and had now abandoned for the past two years. It was said that the halls were ornamented by skulls and antlers of stags. Portraits of the chase and scenes of the Revolutionary War also adorned the hallways. But unlike the high-class atmosphere of its prewar days, a different appearance pervaded the premises. Specifically, in 1863, a virtual city of three thousand former slaves occupied the surrounding grounds. The "city" consisted of refugees from Washington, and they were provided with food, cooking wood, lodging, and schooling for the children. I saw young people my age sitting on logs, the lawn, or wherever they could, eagerly learning some of the same things I was learning in school.

Also, because of the protracted number of war dead, the shortage of burial space in the city, and a species of revenge to its former owner, part of the land became a cemetery. It was rumored that this latter act was done to make sure that the traitor, Lee, would never again have the use of Arlington House as a home. The first to be buried were unknown Confederate soldiers. When the war finally ended, the grounds in front of the mansion was the scene of wild celebration by black folks reminiscent of the celebrations in the city in April 1862 and January 1863 as the former slaves acknowledged the end of the conflict and their final liberation. I could see through a spyglass I had received as a gift from the island in the vicinity of the old animal park black folk dancing all about the lawn. When there was a lull in the bustle of the city, I thought I could hear them singing, "Year of Jubilo," which contained the words;

De massa run, ha ha
De darkey stay, ho ho

It must be now de Kingdom
Comin', in de year ob jubilo

The area they had come from in Washington City was the aforementioned Murder Bay and other contraband camps like Camp Barker at 13th W and S St N. When the war started, the population of the city was a little over sixty thousand. Including the forty thousand former slaves, it increased to two hundred thousand at times during the war.

1960s

June 1961 saw my proficiency on the piano escalate to the point where the teacher, Mr. Jones, was willing to "risk" my participation in a recital. Accordingly, for most of that month, I had to practice the song that he picked out for me to play. During those hot days, I would sit at the piano and practice with the windows open. Thus I was at once able to impress the kids outside playing baseball and be frustrated at not being able to do that which I much preferred over this piano stuff. However, Mom would have none of it. So practice it was. Over and over again I played that song until I learned the lyrics and actually began to like it. Not only did I like it, but it took on a haunting aura, as though this was not the first time I had played it or heard it. I wonder how it came to be that of all of the simple compositions that Mr. Jones could have picked, he chose one that would be so significant to the location where I played it, and moreover, the eventual fascination that I would have with the events that occurred there. Continuously I played the song:

Yes we'll rally 'round the flag boys
We'll rally once again
Shouting the Battle Cry of Freedom
And we'll rally from the hillside
We'll gather from the plain
Shouting the Battle Cry of Freedom
Chorus
The Union forever
Hurrah boys Hurrah
Down with the traitor
And up with the star

I began to play with such fervor that I was sure that someone standing a block away at that fort named Stevens could have heard me. Being on a direct route from school to home, the fort frequently served as a natural site for playing war and soldier after school. We envisioned the great Civil War battle that took place in our neighborhood a century earlier. Our only dilemma was one of, who were Union and who were Rebels. My imagination allowed me to hear that song being gaily sung by US Army engineers as they constructed that fort near the house exactly a hundred summers before.

1860s

In the hot summer weather with our windows wide open, I could hear the sounds of construction of some species of building just a few yards away from our new residence in Washington County. It turned out that this was Fort Massachusetts, one of a ring of sixty-nine forts that would eventually encircle the city.

The good news about this was that it reinforced our confidence that the Rebels would not attack the city anytime soon. However, the news was bad for one of our neighbors, Aunt Betty Thomas. As I said before, we had moved to Vinegar Hill, a part of the Brightwoood section of Washington County where other black families lived, one of whom was Aunt Betty. As it turned out, they had to take her farmland to build the fort. Amid the steady serenade of hammers, saws, and various species of tools was the wailing of the elderly widow as she watched helplessly as they turned her cellar into the magazine for the fort. One day there was much excitement in the neighborhood as the word spread that a tall, lanky figure had emerged from a carriage and then paid avisit to the unfortunate widow. It was none other than President Lincoln, who had made the trip for the specific purpose of comforting the widow. It is said that he conveyed his condolences, appreciation for her sacrifice, and a promise to compensate her in due time all at once.

Meanwhile construction of the fort continued. To lessen the monotony of the work, I could sometimes hear the men gaily sing:

We will rally 'round the flag boys
we'll rally once again
shouting the battle cry of freedom
We will rally from the hillside

We'll gather from the plain
Shouting the Battle Cry of Freedom
Chorus
"The Union forever
Hurrah boys hurrah
Down with the traitor
And up with the star

I was so inspired by those lyrics and melody that I asked Mr. Withers if I might play it as a piano lesson.

Soon there were reports of skirmishes such as Philippi in Western Virginia. This was the first actual land engagement of this conflict. It occurred in June 1861. The newspapers reported that we had won. The next month on the hot Sunday afternoon of July 21, many of the former neighbors and citizens who lived downtown prepared picnic lunches for an excursion into the country. This I understood was for the purpose of watching our soldiers quickly dispatch a bunch of Rebels who were supposedly approaching a railroad junction named Manassas. We had been to the church that day when we saw the crowds as they gaily crossed Long Bridge in their carriages to see the festivities. Before that day was over, however, we saw the same throngs returning to the city more hastily and with much less ceremony than their departure. The reports from those prodigal sons was that the Southerners put a whipping on our boys. The rumors were confirmed as we began to see soldiers wounded and otherwise reposing in doorways, on sidewalks, and on wharves down Sixth Street W and M Street S. The steady influx of soldiers continued into the following day, which was rainy. Some sympathetic ladies set up a table at the corner of Fourteenth Street W and Pennsylvania Avenue in front of their homes, distributing lemonade and other refreshments. Many of these men were grievously wounded in makeshift tents but receiving no medical attention. For the next several days, many of their wounds remained untreated. Some of them died, but many more would have had it not been for that mysterious angel of mercy that I saw at the infirmary and at the Capitol helping those Massachusetts soldiers. Miss Barton again displayed angelic qualities. As could be expected, many of the wounded later succumbed to their wounds. They were buried at a place outside the city on Capitol

N, near that cottage owned by one Mr. Riggs and sometimes used by President Lincoln as a refuge from the summer's heat.

A month after that fiasco out in Manassas, it came to light that it may have been more than coincidence that the Rebels had been so well prepared to meet the US forces under General McDowell. This development first piqued my curiosity when one day—August 23 to be exact—I had gone down to our old neighborhood to see my old chum Crittenden.

While walking down Sixteenth Street, I saw a little girl up in a tree shouting, "Mother's been arrested."

At that moment, the house was being guarded by soldiers and detectives. "Mother," it turns out, was none other than Rose Greenhow, now suspected as being a Confederate spy. She was the same lady that my chum Crittenden was questioned about when that grim-faced man in Lafayette Park held on to the slim hope that the day that Crittenden saw the shawled lady was the day that his wife was at a party at Mrs. Greenhow's house. As explained earlier, this turned out not to be the case. Indeed, she was one of many comely ladies thought to be subversive against our government. Their methods were hardly original as they resorted to no more than the usual feminine method of influencing the judgment of men. Little Rose's arboreal warning was largely for the purpose of alerting fellow spies that this was no longer available as a rendezvous point. We saw the men taking Miss Greenhow to a carriage, ostensibly en route to the Old Capitol Prison on A Street N. We saw her go back inside briefly and emerge again. She probably destroyed some species of evidence when she went inside.

In the midst of such a great conflict, it was difficult to imagine that President Lincoln had any time for a normal existence. His popularity waxed and waned depending on the fortunes of war at any given time. His great burden did allow him time to engage in other activities from time to time. It was relatively easy to see him as his itinerary frequently took him among the citizenry. I managed to see him on some occasions. The first time was as he rode to his summer White House at the cottage on the grounds of the Soldiers Home. The cottage, named Corn Riggs by its owner, Elijah Riggs, the prominent banker, had been for the use of presidents beginning with Buchanan. Its rural setting was conducive to cool summer breezes, a respite from the oppressive heat of Washington

City. The cottage had two front gables and four chimneys and was of a yellowish hue. In front was a carriageway shaped like a figure eight with a flagpole in the middle of it. It was next door to the main castle-like building on the grounds. A second cottage on the grounds was used by Secretary Stanton and his family. Generally the Lincoln family remained during the hot months while the president journeyed back and forth to the White House. It was on the commutes that one could see the lone, tall figure on horseback, which struck an interesting silhouette against the glow of a summer twilight as he made his way to the cottage.

There was a general concern over his safety. This was particularly true among us black folk, for we knew that if any harm came to him, there was no telling as to what the fate of our people would be if in the hands of Vice President Hannibal Hamlin or the president's enemies in Congress. Occasionally, these fears were realized, such as the time in 1862 that a bullet pierced his tall top hat while he was on the way to the Soldier's Home. He, however, was no worse for wear in that his chief complaint regarding that situation was the damage to his hat. We heard that Mr. Lincoln kept an envelope in a pigeonhole in his desk that contained some eighty death threats. He had marked this envelope "assassination." After the shooting incident in 1862, he would make his journeys around town in the company of a cavalry squad.

While his popularity fluctuated generally, an event in the spring of 1862 virtually locked him into eternal greatness among black folk in Washington City and the surrounding area. Thursday, April 16, 1862, was a jubilant time for African Americans in the District of Columbia, for on this day President Lincoln signed a document ending slavery in the entire jurisdiction. Some said that the president had some reservations about taking this bold step and that he had contemplated vetoing the bill. However, both houses of Congress had passed it, and a veto would likely not be advantageous politically for him. It is still likely that he was ultimately pleased to see the peculiar institution abolished in the capital, as evidenced by the comment accompanying his signature on the bill that he had "ever desired to see the national capital freed from the institution in some satisfactory way."[26] I was downtown at the Centre Market on

---

[26] Benjamin Quarles, *Lincoln and the Negro* (DaCapo Press, Boston, Massachusetts, 1991).

an errand and saw countless black folks celebrating in all manner of gyrations in the street. This jubilation was not reserved exclusively for the blacks of Washington. Mother's sister and brothers in Baltimore and New York, respectively, wrote of similar celebrations by our race in those cities. Baltimore set May 1 and New York set May 5 aside as days of public celebration for the event. Back in Washington City, on Sunday, April 20, every black church, including ours, held a day of prayer and celebration.[27] For the next several weeks, I also saw countless former slaveholders in endless lines at the circuit court—the same one on Indiana Avenue where that grim-faced man was tried—applying for the compensation offered them by the government. It was my understanding from school and the newspapers that each slaveholder was to be awarded up to $300 per slave. This bounty, however, was only available if the claimant swore allegiance to the Union in the present war of rebellion. I am certain that there were three categories of claimant here. One was the true loyalist who felt that just compensation warranted separation from his human chattel. The second was the secessionist whose greed outweighed his integrity and who quite cheerfully accepted the offered bounty and quite hypocritically took the oath of allegiance. The third was the diehard rebel to whom no amount of money would shake his belief that the white race had the right to dominate and own the black race. He would rather die in the last ditch than give up his slaves, notwithstanding a handsome monetary reward.

Access to the money offered by the government did not come easily, however. The prospective claimant had ninety days to present a claim to one of three commissioners appointed by President Lincoln. The claim had to consist of a list every person ostensibly held in bondage by the claimant, including the name, age, physical description, and manner of acquisition of the person. The claims were to be reviewed for the next nine months to determine if all conditions had been met. However, even before this claim was presented, virtually the same information had to be provided to the clerk of the circuit for the District of Columbia. If a prospective claimant failed to do any one of these steps, he would not be paid. The advantages to this new act of the Congress was not confined to slaveholders. The act also provided for voluntary emigration of those former slaves to colonies

---

[27] Ibid.

outside the United States, with an incentive of a hundred dollars per person to those who would volunteer to leave.

To us free persons of color, the celebration in the streets was somewhat academic. However, Father and Mother both saw overall good for our race, slave or free. Strangely enough, there were also parallels to the Fugitive Slave Act insofar as danger to free blacks was concerned. Like the act of 1850, this new emancipation act invited fraud at the expense of the liberty of free persons of color. It took little imagination to envision some fiend seizing a free person of color, temporarily enslaving him, and making claims under the act for compensation in exchange for his "emancipation." Father warned me of this potential danger. More pertinent to the newly freed slaves was the potential compensation under the law of the district. These eventualities were taken seriously, notwithstanding the fact that the law itself proposed a penalty of five to twenty years in prison for anyone guilty of such conduct. A related problem with equally devastating effect was also born of this emancipation in the District of Columbia. Hearing of this situation, many bondsmen in neighboring Maryland and Virginia would fly to Washington in an effort to find freedom. This fact naturally invited efforts by slave owners in those two states to come to the city for the purpose of recapturing their property. However, this endeavor, as could be expected, crossed over into the area of random kidnapping of black residents of the district who had never been slaves at all or at least not in Maryland or Virginia. This phenomenon continued even after the president later freed slaves in the Confederacy the following year. By then the situation was urgent enough to prompt the provost marshal of the War Department to write to the president and outline the current state of affairs regarding this problem. Colonel L. C. Becker informed the president that armed bands of slave owners regularly came into the city and indiscriminately, fiercely assailed men, women, and children slaves and shot, beat, and imprisoned them for shipment to slave jurisdictions. It was reported that at least forty people had been killed in this manner, of whom three of the bodies lay in the woods within view of the president's house. A particular account was given of an incident in which a band of such marauders surrounded the house of a free black woman and broke into the house and forcibly took away three free blacks. It was also reported that two young girls in the city were chained in the garret of a private home and beaten mercilessly with a trace chain. There was no indication of any response to this letter by the president. Mother and Father were always wary of this impending danger and warned me accordingly. Perhaps actions taken by the president on September 24, 1862, was a subtle if not direct response to these occurrences and other issues as well. On that day, he declared martial law in the city so that lawbreakers of this time and others who displayed disloyalty to the Union could be dealt with without the formalities of due process. We black folks were rather used to that method already

While the nation was in the midst of this crisis, my new love for the game of baseball was undaunted. When Father used to take me to see the Potomacs and Nationals at age seven, most of my interest in the game was the fact that I was somewhere with Father. But now this game was a part of my very fiber. I would read the *Washington Star* and the *National Intelligencer* each day during the warm time of year to learn the fate of the Nationals or the Potomacs. Both teams had gotten their start as the result of various government clerks forming teams in 1859. The Nationals officially were called the National Baseball Club of Washington, D. C. They had a thrower named Arthur Pue Gorman who later became a US senator. I had no idea how long this team would exist, but I somehow surmised that his official status in government would somehow come to be associated with this team in the long run. Referring to the Potomacs, the *Washington Star* in 1859 stated, "It is good to see health-promoting exercises taking the place of insipid enervating amusements."

Later, in 1872, the Nationals became a member of the National Association of Baseball Players, which was represented by twenty-five cities. Prior to 1869, these teams consisted of young men playing purely for the love of the game inasmuch as pay was never considered. In the case of the Nationals, as with the Potomacs, many of the players were government workers looking for a diversion from their regular routine. Frequently the Nationals' performance would evoke tears from me and on rare occasions, joy. On those joyous occasions, it became clear that the games, though prosecuted vigorously, were not cutthroat affairs but a gentleman's game of sorts. The Nationals even had a constitution that called for the payment of dues at fifty cents initially and twenty-five cents monthly. Fines would be assessed at ten cents for foul language, twenty-five cents for disputing the umpire's call, and ten cents for expressing a contrary opinion on a close call prior to the umpire's call.

On some occasions, the Potomacs and Nationals would play each other. The Potomacs' home was the White Lot, a field just south of the president's house. On May 5, 1860, the two teams met at that place.

Father took me there where we saw the Potomacs triumph 35–15. The large number of scores was likely due to the striker being able to dictate to the thrower where he wanted the ball.[28] The following month, the Nationals avenged this setback 46–14. The Nationals continued to play during the Great War though the Potomacs seemed to have played out. By the summer of 1865, the Nationals had established a rivalry with the Atlantic of Brooklyn, the Athletic of Philadelphia, and the Excelsiors of Brooklyn. During one game, Father and I, along with six thousand others, saw President Johnson in top hat, witnessing the action on the White Lot.

I was near the National Hotel on July 2, 1866, when I saw men of the Nationals enter following a contest, followed by their vanquished foes, the Athletic of Philadelphia, for dinner. After several toasts, the players took their repast of spring chicken, tongue croquettes, and lobster salad.

At our dinner Father would frequently have to curtail my endless discussion of baseball. At school we played the game fervently. The thrower had to cross his legs before throwing the ball in an underhanded manner. His other hand had to be behind his back. An umpire would sometimes be assigned at our games but would refrain from calling balls and strikes but would encourage the striker to swing at well-thrown balls. But if the umpire believed the striker was consistently passing at well-thrown balls, he had an option of calling the striker dead. The striker was required to keep the bat on his shoulder until he swung. I was particularly efficient at playing in the outer field. Although the rules allowed that a striker was dead if a ball was caught in flight or on the first hop, I was frequently able to catch the ball before it hit the ground. While in the capacity of striker, except for the time that Father scolded me about my striking style, I was able to discern the difference between balls that were well thrown and otherwise. The rules did not allow for walks. If the thrower continued to

---

[28] A "behind" was the nineteenth century term for the catcher, a "striker" was the batter, the "thrower" was the pitcher, and a "dead" was an out.

throw balls that should have been swung at, the umpire could penalize the striker for not swinging.

The New York rules, as practiced by their 1845 team the Knickerbockers, required that the bases be ninety feet apart and the thrower's position to be forty-five feet from home plate. It had also been established that three strikes at a pitched ball made a dead and that the other team would come to bat after the batting team made three deads. There was no set number of players on the field and no limitation as to the times teams came to be strikers had been set. This version of the game had been first played in Hoboken, New Jersey in 1846. Newspaper accounts in the '50s showed these players in their knicker pants ready to strike a thrown ball. The field was manicured with a dirt line between the pitcher and home base. We even heard that our unfortunate soldiers who fell into Rebel hands as prisoners whiled their time away at such places as the Salisbury prison camp in North Carolina and the Danville prison camp in Virginia while playing this game. It was prosecuted most vigorously despite the heat of summer in all quarters. I hear the Rebels were doing the same thing at Johnson's Island in Lake Erie and Camp Douglas in Chicago. I particularly remember 1862, when the Nationals frequently defeated the Athletic of Philadelphia. They would play at Nationals Grounds, on beautiful grounds just south of the president's mansion. Holly Hollingshead was a striker who would frequently avoid deads, and Ed Mincher would be called dead after failing to strike three well-thrown balls. The field had no outer boundary save the ring of spectators in the outer field. There were several African Americans on some of the teams. Many of them learned to play the game while confined in prison camps when they were lucky enough to have been captured by the Confederates. But this issue of the capture of black troops by the Confederates is the subject of an entire separate treatise regarding this great war. But my goal at this stage in my life was to become a member of the National Association of Baseball Players, which in 1860 had sixty teams. This organization had been founded in 1858 with twenty-five clubs. Father told me that hitherto there had been no formal restriction against black baseball players but that it would be hard to gauge the state of affairs when I became of age to play. In fact, by 1871 when I was a young man, the game had turned into a professional one, in which players were being paid. The National Association of Professional Baseball Players took the lead in this endeavor. The Philadelphia Pythians were rejected from entry into this league because of events in December 1867. Indeed, true to Father's prediction, at that time, officials of the National Association of Baseball Players voted to preclude black men, which gave rise to Negro Leagues. Prominent among these teams were the Philadelphia Excelsiors and the Brooklyn Uniques. They played for the Negro Championship in October 1867 after the Excelsiors had paraded around the field prior to the game with fife and drum. This game had seized the country so ardently that men were willing to pay large sums of money to have players engage in this exciting pastime. In 1869, the Cincinnati Red Stockings had turned into a professional franchise, paying its players. Washington had another team called the Olympics founded by one Nicholas Young in 1871 and were members of the National Association of Baseball Players. Other teams in Washington were the Interiors, the Unions, the Jeffersons, and the Capitals. Capitalizing on the new trend of paying players, Young founded a new league in 1876 called the National League of Professional Baseball Players. Many predicted that this league would last well into the next century. But black men were not allowed to play in some leagues. Bud Fowler, a behind, of Cooperstown, New York, where the game was reputedly invented, and Fleet Walker were prominent black men on white teams, the latter player on the Toledo Mud Hens of a new league called the American Association, becoming the first black major leaguer. Fowler would play gallantly without mitt or protection of his chest. The Olympics played at the Olympic Grounds located at. Among my favorite players were Doug Allison, a behind, and Henry Burroughs, an outfielder. One of Mother's brothers who eventually was called to be a soldier and captured at Salisbury wrote and told us that at prison camp, black prisoners were frequently chosen for teams because of their ball-handling ability.

1960s

Among my favorite players on the Senators were Bob Allison and Jeff Burroughs, both outfielders. Don Mincher would frequently strike out, failing to strike three well-thrown balls, and becoming dead is what it would have been referred to in the old days, like his predecessor a century earlier. Other players were Jim Lemon, Earl Battey, and Chuck Hinton. On Saturday August 20, 1960, Dad and I went to Griffith Stadium where we saw the Senators squander a lead late in the game against the hated Yankees. A potentially game-winning ground ball found its way through the legs of shortstop Billy Consolo. This opened the gates for a 5-4 Senator win to quickly devolve into a 9-5 Yankee win.

Back on the national front, in the fall of 1962, additional shots were taken in that war between the United States and Russia. This situation had now escalated from rockets to the moon to Russian rockets situated just ninety miles from American shores in Cuba. Moreover, the *Washington Post* said that they were aimed at certain American cities, one of which was Washington. Well, this threat caused people Mom and Dad's age to conjure up thoughts of Pearl Harbor as the last time America was attacked. The real old-timers were making reference to some long-ago summertime attack of Washington by an "unreconstructed" Confederate general named Jubal A. Early. Apparently back in 1864, this man was literally a block away from the current location of our house and made a serious threat on the Union capital during the Civil War. There was much talk of nuclear war with all its horrors now in 1962. The Russian leader Nikita Khrushchev was literally testing the resolve of this young President Kennedy. The question of the day was, "What will Kennedy do?" From the study of science in class, I understood all too well what the all the horrors of nuclear war were if carried to their logical conclusion. Ultimately a war between the United States and Russia could have resulted in a chunk of the earth being literally blown away. This was a horrible thought to be sure. However, in the mind of a ten-year-old, the thought of a war took on an air of excitement. After all, we boys in the neighborhood spent a substantial amount of time playing army. It was obvious, however, that this was not looked at as a game by the grownups. Sometime in October of that year, 1962, President Kennedy issued an ultimatum to the Russians: remove the missiles from Cuba or risk nuclear war with the United States. As an added measure, I seem to recall the president mounting missiles in Turkey that were aimed at Moscow, Kiev, or Leningrad. The next thing we knew, reports were in that Soviet ships were taking several dismantled missiles back across the Atlantic. This was but another battle in this cold war, as it was called. Dad worked overtime atr the Pentagon during this time of crisis. His position was a trying one because the unexpected insofar as security was concerned continuously lurked around every corner. With the determined and courageous efforts of the Kennedy administration, it appeared that the country, and indeed the city, were saved. Dad liked to take, and we gave him, credit for his contribution to that effort.

The other skirmishes continued on after this Cuban missile crises, largely in the area of the space race. Not to be outdone by Yuri Gagarin and the Russians, Kennedy matched his feat three weeks afterward by sending Alan Shepherd into space aboard the Freedom 7. Gus Grissom did the same thing in the Liberty Bell 7 in July 1961. Somehow the capsule filled with water, and he had to do some swimming to survive. By the beginning of 1963, four Americans had been in space.

In this war with Russia, the Americans were slightly ahead. Casualties of this war were the crew of the nuclear submarine *Thresher,* which went down for the final time in the North Atlantic in April 1963. The teacher explained that while the cause of its sinking was unclear, the fate of the men was clear. We were familiar with the term *explosion,* but in the explanation of what happened to the crew at the bottom of the ocean, the teacher taught us the word *implosion.* In other words, the tons of pressure at the depths of the ocean crushed the submarine and its crew.

On that New Year's Day, there was celebration of the hundredth anniversary of the Emancipation Proclamation. The timing of that celebration was good because the international issues involving Russia were actually secondary to the domestic strife brewing at home over the issue of race. Here it was a hundred years after the release from bondage of African Americans in this city as well as the United States, and yet bitter conflicts were still present. A good man named Martin Luther King Jr. had been striving for the past decade or so to end segregation and discrimination against blacks in this country. Except for the absence of a bona fide declaration of war, this situation was not unlike that which this country endured exactly a hundred years before. It appeared now that black Americans were fighting for rights that the war fought a century earlier was to have secured. Instead of battlefields named Shiloh, Antietam, or Gettysburg, the battles were fought in Greensboro, Birmingham, Montgomery, and Jackson. There would be daily reports of how protesters both black and white were beaten by the police or set upon by police dogs and high-powered water hoses. For the most part, the Kennedy administration denounced this type of treatment and advocated for equal rights for all people. In that regard he approved of a tremendous protest arranged by King and many other civil rights leaders scheduled for Washington in the summer of 1963. When that day came, Kennedy still supported it, despite coping with the personal tragedy of the death of two-day-old Patrick Bouvier Kennedy being born on August 7 and dying on August 9, 1963. Thereafter, Mrs. Kennedy made no public appearances until November 22, 1963.

1860s

As 1862 dawned, things did not look particularly good for the Union and the president. On February 20, things got even worse for the president personally. On this date twelve-year-old Willie Lincoln succumbed to typhoid fever. The president is said to have stated, "I know he is in a better place. But then again we loved him so. It is hard, hard to have him die." Despite his personal loss, the president continued to prosecute the war. Though still officially at the helm of the country, the Lincolns, particularly the first lady, made no public personal appearances after Willie's death in the form of dinner parties, though they would occasionally go to the theatre.

After that Union debacle in Manassas, it became obvious to everyone that this was not going to be a quick war. Three months after that, the Union was again defeated at Balls Bluff, several miles up the Potomac from Washington City. The defeat was worsened by the fact that many of our soldiers drowned in a futile attempt to retreat across the Potomac in the face of the Rebel onslaught. Weeks later bodies were still coming ashore downstream in Washington. One was caught on the pilings of Long Bridge and others at the Sixth Street Wharf. A young lieutenant who had been at Harvard with the president's son, Robert, and had left to join the army was wounded through the lungs there. I got a glimpse of him later near our house in another battle. His name was Oliver Wendell Holmes. I understand he was brought to Washington to recover from his wounds. Sometime during this period, he became enamored with a young lady named Lucy Hale, the daughter of Senator Hale. The gossip had it that he had a rival for her affection in the form an upcoming Shakespearean actor—the same one that got sick watching John Brown hang.

The Union reverses added fuel to the applications made by men like

Frederick Douglass and others to Mr. Lincoln to allow black men to fight. When the opportunity arose, it was pointed out to the president that his counterpart, Jefferson Davis, freely used slaves to support the Confederate armies in the form of cooks, teamsters, and the construction of fortifications. The absurdity of the situation where the enemy had made involuntary use of a class of people to the disadvantage of the Union and the present administration's refusal for political reasons to do the same with people who were all too willing to help was pointed out. In addition to the public, the president had to listen to an outspoken colleague and old friend from Kentucky who needled him constantly about his failure to use black troops and possible emancipation of slaves for that purpose. He was currently the emissary to Russia and vehemently opposed slavery. His name was Cassius Marcellus Clay. Although it may have seemed so, Douglass's and Clay's clamor was not falling on deaf ears. The president seemed to be thinking along those lines anyway, though not publicly so stating. This was first manifested in conjunction with another personal tragedy of another member of the president's administration. The Secretary of War Stanton also had the misfortune of losing a child to death. At the funeral on Sunday July 13, 1862, he first broached the subject of emancipation of the slaves to cabinet members Gideon Welles, navy, and William Seward, state. Nine days later, he made the general announcement at the cabinet meeting. Word was that he had actually written a draft of this document but at the behest of Secretary Seward placed it in a desk drawer pending a Union victory, ensuring that the document would be sent forth from a position of strength. He sure did not get that victory exactly a month later on August 22 because the rebels defeated him again at the same place where they had so unceremoniously run all of those soldiers and civilians back to Washington last summer. In fact, on that very day he was still taking a rather neutral public position on the matter. The *Star* quoted him as saying on that day, "If I could save the Union by freeing all of the slaves I would. If I could save the Union by freeing none of the slaves I would. If I could save the Union by freeing some of the slaves and leaving the others alone I would." Like most people, white, black, slave, and free, two other prominent proponents of the abolition of slavery and the induction of black troops were not aware of the president's now-progressive thinking. They were Governors Curtin and Andrew of

Pennsylvania and Massachusetts, respectively. Even as the president waited for this victory, these two statesmen were planning to meet with him in Altoona, Pennsylvania, to discuss the aforementioned topic. However, on September 22, 1862, the president obviated the need for such a meeting by informing that pair of his plans to wait for a victory.

1960s

Perhaps I had not thought too much about the experiences I had in the '50s with respect to discriminatory practices against black Americans. This could have been because I was entrenched in a middle-class life, being taught all of the values of mainstream America, believing that I was a part of it. To some extent, I probably was. However, as could be seen from the protests in the South and the agitation among black leaders, this was not grossly the case among members of my race. The evils of this country were being daily brought to the forefront. The August 1963 March on Washington was just the beginning of an era of protest over the treatment of blacks in the United States. In the fall of 1962, the sixth-grade teacher, Mrs. Mullaly, began to talk about an American boxer who was about to fight an Englishman by the name of Henry Cooper. Dad and I watched fights on television and I was somewhat of a boxing aficionado, but for some reason, I had never heard of this guy. She mimicked how his intentions were to win with his fists but that, failing to obtain victory by that method, he would surely win with his mouth. This man also displayed a sense of pride for his race and from what anyone could gather was a major force in this social movement known as civil rights for blacks. Well this man defeated this Henry Cooper amid the jeers and hostile gestures of Cooper's countrymen in London. This fighter then earned a shot at the heavyweight title against one Charles "Sonny" Liston on February 25, 1964. Against overwhelming odds, he defeated Liston that night as Mom and I and most of the nation listened on radio from Miami when Liston refused to answer the bell for round seven of that fight. The new champion immediately proclaimed himself the king and the greatest, not neglecting to note that after the fight he was "still pretty." Given his new stature as heavyweight champ, his political assertions were given even greater weight than before. He was yet another voice that the current administration now under President Lyndon B. Johnson listened to and perhaps influenced him to push for a momentous piece of legislation, not unlike that which was put forth almost exactly a century before. The legislation was the Civil Rights Act of 1964, and the boxer who had contributed to the overall clamor was Cassius Marcellus Clay, named after another prominent Kentuckian of the last century.

Prior to that act being passed, it had been rumored that Congress under President Johnson would do something to alleviate the plight of black Americans. It was the general consensus that President Kennedy's administration had been a benevolent one for our people, but the jury was still out with respect to the Texan Johnson, who had previously voted against a similar act while a member of congress. The seven-month period between November 1963 and July 1964 was one in which Americans generally and black Americans particularly were in suspense. Finally on July 1, it was announced and passed. This was truly a pivotal time in the fate pf black Americans, not unlike that which existed exactly a hundred years before.

But contemporaneously with this domestic concern loomed an international matter some twelve thousand miles away. The American objective of curbing the spread of communism had resulted in military personnel being sent to the southeastern Asian country of Vietnam. Throughout the remainder of the 1960s and into the 1970s the conflict wore on, dividing Americans on what our role should be there, if any.

During this tumultuous period nationally also came the personal tumultuous period personally called adolescence. By the mid-1960s, the good fortune that I have frequently referred to earlier of having parents with positive values that reinforced my ability to ultimately succeed in life produced an independently thinking, reasonably intelligent person in myself. The logical outcome of this seems to have been one of mutual respect for my feelings and opinions notwithstanding my youth. However, this proved to be in opposition to the mind-set of my parents, whose attitude toward children was more closely akin to that of parents in the last century (i.e., children's opinions did not count). Theirs was not as unreasonable an attitude as that of previous generations, but it was close. Consequently, the usual emotions and conflicts between the generations were present in our household.

1860s

Washington was now a bona fide wartime city. The *Washington Star* reported that many thousands of soldiers in and around the city were supplied by more than seven thousand prostitutes. Most of them solicited on the streets, while the others worked in more than 450 houses of ill-fame in the city. Along with the "fallen women" came confidence men, gamblers, thieves, pickpockets, and many other undesirable characters. They contributed to the statistics outlined in the typical quarterly police arrest reports mentioned earlier. The focal point of most of this shady conduct was an area south of Pennsylvania Avenue and east of Fourteenth Street W known as Murder Bay. Most of the aforementioned brothels were centered in this vicinity. Adding to the notoriety of this locale was the fact that most of forty thousand former slaves who found their way into the city settled in this area. Obviously their unfortunate circumstances could only exacerbate the criminal activity that occurred here. Running through this area was Ohio Avenue, the site of several houses of ill-repute, including Nellie Starr's and Mrs. Venable's place. Nellie Starr's daughter was enamored with that same actor who vied for the affections of Lucy Hale. She apparently worked in the profession but made news later because of her reaction to the actions of that same actor later on.[29] Gambling establishments and canterburies were also found here. One particular canterbury was on the south side of the avenue between Ninth and Tenth Street W. It had the word "CANTERBURY" emblazoned on the western front. By day there was a sea of horses and wagons on the side of it because of its proximity to the market. This innocent exterior belied the events

---

[29] Young Miss Starr had to be revived for self-imposed chloroform poisoning upon learning that her J. W. Booth was implicated in the death of the president.

on the inside. As a young man, it killed me not to be allowed inside. The loud singing of the calliope only added to my torture. On summer nights the smoke and sounds emerged from the open windows even more prominently. With the loud noise and cheers apparently arising from the actions of the females inside and the almost certainly fabricated experience of some of my contemporaries claimed to have had when they went inside, it was close to inhumane to be denied ingress. I could see the countenances of men emerging from this place on any given night and know that I was indeed being deprived of my rightful pleasure. On a particular occasion when I was twelve or thirteen years old, I even saw the rascal that Mr. Withers alluded to as a friend of the family of that talented boy, Sousa, emerging from the canterbury late at night with a character with a rodent-like face. Both men would do something to refresh my recollection of them in the coming months. Alas, denied I was. I remember seeing an article in the *Washington Star* of a soldier being knocked "flat-horizontal" on Ohio Avenue. By far, however, crime was not limited to this seedy area of the city. Indeed, the Island and Nigger Hill were equally notorious. Police described much of the city as one of "crime, filth, and poverty." Examples of the problem of crime were outlined in the aforementioned quarterly police reports. There were, however, still some respectable establishments like Harvey's Oyster House and Gautier's French Restaurant. These were located primarily on the north side of Pennsylvania Avenue. In the winter and spring of 1865, I would sometimes see that actor named Booth dining inside Gautier's. The stature of that establishment was befitting the likes of Booth. But what puzzled me was the times that I saw him with that rodent-looking character I would see emerging from the Canterbury. Why would Booth possibly want to dine with an unkempt, malodorous person as he, who was conspicuously out of place there? Later I would sometimes begin to see Booth with other men, including that rascal that Mr. Withers told me about.

Back in the '50s, it was mentioned that young boys a little older than I dropped out of school to work at the Navy Yard and the arsenal. The latter edifice had an interesting past and as it would turn out, an even more interesting future. It had been constructed in 1836 at Greenleaf Point and started out as the first and a model federal penitentiary. Later a portion of it was used to store munitions of war. With the current wartime situation, the president determined that there was a need to store more munitions and accordingly had all of the prisoners moved to a prison in Albany, New York. During this period of war, the aforementioned employment of young boys occurred with greater regularity and expanded to include many women. Mother was among those at the Navy Yard. I thank the Almighty that she was not among those at the arsenal. Friday, June 17, 1864, dawned like a typical summer day in Washington. Hot! But it was destined to be anything but typical. Some one hundred ladies, mostly Irish immigrants in their twenties, engaged in the production of black powder for the balls used in our army rifles. As is usual in the summer heat, the windows were open per direction of Mr. Brown, the superintendent of the arsenal. It all started just before noon, when a pan in the southeast corner window containing fireworks for the upcoming July 4 celebration caught fire. This was blamed on heat from the intense sunlight. Sparks promptly flew out of the pan and landed in the powder, where the ladies were rolling cartridges. I saw on that day horse-drawn, steam-driven water wagons from one of the many volunteer fire companies rushing down Fourth and a Half Street toward the arsenal. Conspicuous among the vehicles was a relatively new steam fire engine brought from the Hibernia Company of Philadelphia on September 15, 1862. It had been employed by a new federal firefighting force, which replaced the volunteers. Perhaps not coincidentally, two weeks after the tragedy at the arsenal, the first paid fire departments came about to serve the city. I eventually found my way to the arsenal, where crowds composed primarily relatives of the victims were already there. The firemen were gallantly taking control of the blaze. I have always conjectured as to how many of those young ladies could have been saved had this conflagration occurred just a fortnight later when in that exact time frame, the paid fire department for Washington City would have been available. Many of the girls were burned to a crisp and beyond recognition. Those who were not completely burned presented only a trunk, the appendages somehow missing. One girl had every stitch of clothes burned from her except her gaiter shoes. It was speculated that some of the debris fell around her feet, thus preventing her lower body from catching fire.

That Sunday, June 19, I saw a sad procession headed out of the city to that cemetery where Teresa and Barton used to meet. It was in this procession that I got my first good look at perhaps the saddest mourner in that procession. The tall, lanky figure that had been carrying the weight of this terrible war on his shoulders for the last three years rode with Secretary Stanton in one of 150 carriages to the cemetery. Some two thousand of us were located at both the arsenal and the cemetery to hear Father A. Bokel of St. Dominick's Church give last rites. It was a truly sad day in the capital, brightened only by news that earlier that day three thousand miles to the east the notorious Confederate raider *Alabama* was now resting comfortably at the bottom of the English Channel. The word was that the USS *Kersarge* had caught up with it off the coast of Calais, France, and with hundreds of Frenchmen, including the painter Claude Monet observing, had sent the notorious ship to the bottom. Father was particularly happy because a black sailor named Joachim Pease had been a gunner on the *Kersarge*. It was our hope that he had been instrumental in our success. As it were, he was one of several black sailors to earn the Medal of Honor in this terrible war. When Secretary of Navy Gideon Welles returned to his office on Monday, he was greeted by a huge victory flag hanging from the Navy Department façade.

Crowds of another sort were in and about the White House grounds during this general time period. The long-awaited Negro Sunday school picnic took place at the invitation of the president. The scene here vividly illustrated Mother's favorite theme of the difference between black folk of some means as compared to those of a lower class. Fancy carriages, gay bonnets, and fine suits were liberally displayed by those attending the picnic and contrasted with the chestnut brown, torn clothing of the contraband element that sat on the curbsides on Pennsylvania Avenue gazing longingly at the gayety inside the White House grounds. Little was left to their imagination in knowing that they were not accepted by their more affluent fellow Negroes.

Heretofore, the raging war that had wreaked havoc on war-ravaged Virginia, Tennessee and Louisiana had spared Washington City. That is until the summer of 1864 when it all changed. By living in the rural area north of the city and near Maryland, we denizens of Brightwood and Vinegar Hill were the first to learn that something ominous was afoot. Then we saw tremendous dust clouds on the Seventh Street Road as we saw terrified farmers flying desperately in their wagons and on foot toward the city. These were mostly black folks whose conveyances seemed to contain all of their worldly possessions. Father asked one gentleman what the urgency was all about. His panicked response was that, "De Rebels is all over de place 'round Frederick." Presently, we could hear the muffled report of artillery coming from the north being carried on a light summer breeze. On this hot Saturday, July 9, 1864, other landowners like Mr. Benedict Jost and Mr. B. T. Swart were already spreading news of a battle taking place along a river called Monocacy about forty miles north of the city. We later learned that some twelve thousand Confederates under General Jubal A. Early were met by half as many Union men under General Lew Wallace who had without orders, deployed out from Baltimore to meet the threat. By and by, the gun thunder to the north desisted and the question was whether the Rebels were sent scattering like the Romans of old in those chariots or that they were now proceeding to take Baltimore or Washington.[30] We did not learn the outcome of the battle right away but it was reported that by evening, the Confederates were marching down the Georgetown Pike.[31] This intelligence could be discerned by the signal tower at Fort Reno on the other side of Rock Creek from our house. The gallant Wallace, with his inferior numbers, had to retreat back to Baltimore leaving the road to Washington wide open. However, he managed to cause the Rebels lose a valuable day in their quest for Washington. The soldiers at Reno gauged the approach of the enemy by the ever reliable cloud of dust that an advancing army invariably made on the dusty roads. We boys became excited about the prospect of a battle for the city as though it were some romanticized event as seen in ancient Roman or Greek artwork. The grownups were in no way enamored by this prospect given the tendency of the Rebels to destroy homes, take livestock and, for us black folks, take us!

However, Father saw this as a chance to rectify the earlier rejection by the War Department of able-bodied black men for service to the country. He immediately joined the ranks of the War Department clerks, one hundred day men, invalids and USCTs deployed from other fortifications around the city to garrison Fort Stevens near our house. The strength of

---

[30] The Georgetown Pike is now Rockville Pike, which becomes Wisconsin Avenue as it enters the city.

[31] The chariot allusion refers to the fact the Union commander at the battle of Monocacy, General Lew Wallace, wrote *Ben Hur: A Tale of the Christ,* after the war in 1880.

the fortification was relatively weak initially because it was believed that any attack would come down the Georgetown Pike which was protected by the formidable Fort Reno.

Meanwhile, more families were fleeing down the Seventh Street road past the home of Mayor Emery. Mother and I remained put, confident that Father and the other gallant men in the fort would protect us. Other families remained as well, confident that the thrust of the attack would not be at Fort Stevens. This bravado remained in place until we heard news from Mr. Carberry that the ever reliable cloud of dust indicator had shifted according to the garrison at Fort Reno. From that place along the Georgetown Pike the Army Signal Corps had an optimal view well into adjacent Montgomery County, Maryland and noted the cloud of dust veer from the Georgetown Pike, past Mr. Vier's mill. This could have meant only one thing; the Rebels were coming down the Seventh Street Road now protected only by the feebly manned Fort Stevens. Thus ended the day on July 10, 1864.

But on the morrow, the community of Brightwood feasted its collective eyes on another cloud of dust, this one coming from the south, up the Seventh St Road. I heard Mr. Swart excitedly exclaim, "It's the Old Sixth." As it turned out, given the alarm in the city, General Grant had deployed elements of the Sixth Corps

of the Army of the Potomac from the siege of Petersburg and Richmond to save the city. The timing of this event was impeccable as the vanguard of the Rebel army was presently occupying a tulip tree on Mr. Carberry's property for use as a snipers nest and were presently picking off the men in Fort Stevens. This clearly heightened our concern for Father. Mother and I retreated to the cellar where, through a window, we could survey the landscape in front of the fort. On the morning of July 11, 1864, we could see that Union pickets had deployed in our front yard and they were exchanging sharp gunfire with Rebel pickets who were in the rear of the house. We were startled when a bullet pierced one of the upstairs windows. Then we smelled the smoke of battle, which seemed a little more than that of gunpowder. "Oh, God," Mother exclaimed. "Our own good Union men are burning our neighbor's houses." I assured Mother by telling her that I remember Father telling me that sometimes armies have to destroy property of those they are protecting to keep it out of enemy hands. It appeared that the enemy was commandeering barns and houses in the neighborhood for use as snipers nests. Thus the destruction taking place would be beneficial in the long run. The gunfire subsided that evening at the same rate as the daylight until finally both were gone.

The next morning saw renewed fighting and a Rebel advance right behind our house. This advance was arrested by Union infantry rushing through our front yard to greet them along with direct artillery fire from Stevens and enfilading fire from DeRussy and Slocum. From our cellar retreat we could make out sights and sounds from Fort Stevens. Though we could not see Father, we could clearly see another father of sorts: Father Abraham, as the president had come to be known as. I was sure that it was him, but I could not believe that he would have exposed himself to enemy fire as he was doing. I obviously was not the only one who perceived the foolhardiness of this behavior. I presently could see a young lieutenant grab the president and pull him down from the parapet of the fort all the while admonishing him to, "Get down, you damn fool!" Almost immediately, a major who had been standing near the president took a ball from a Rebel sharpshooter and appeared to have been killed. Ironically, the president's benefactor that day had been a classmate of the president's eldest son, Robert Todd Lincoln, at Harvard College, having interrupted his studies to help save the country. In later years, the lieutenant became famous in the field of law as I understood it.

The lieutenant had seen previous action and wounded severely at the battle of Balls Bluff in October, 1861. He also was John Wilkes Booth's and Robert Lincoln's rival suitor of Lucy Hale, daughter of Senator John Preston Hale of Maine. After the war he became Chief Justice of the US Supreme Court and decided a famous negligence case in which he coined the phrase "Stop, Look and Listen" when crossing railroad tracks. He was Oliver Wendell Holmes.

Now skirmishing on July 12 turned into full scale combat as the thrust of the Confederate forces had arrived in nearby Silver Spring near the property of the Blair family. More Union infantry composed largely of the Sixth Corp advanced form the fort and set of a line of battle directly in front of our house. Sharp fighting continued all around our house that entire day. Our gallant men literally held the line because we never saw any Rebels advance past our house. Once again darkness curtailed the unpleasantness and we wondered with great apprehension what the morrow would bring. On the morning of the 13th, we heard no more shooting and saw no Rebels. We cautiously emerged from our safe haven to see several Union and Rebel dead all around the neighborhood. I heard shouting from various people saying," The Rebs have retreated. The city is saved." As it were, they had indeed gone back up the Seventh Street Road but not before pillaging and burning the mansion of Attorney Montgomery Blair, near his father's estate called Silver Spring. I always wondered if they targeted the son's estate rather than the father's which was more opulent I heard. Piecing bits of information that I heard together, I concluded that one Confederate general was familiar with a wine cellar in the home of the elder Blair, a fact that he came to know from visits to the house while he served as Vice-President of the United States under President Buchannan. This was John C. Breckenridge, whose candidacy contributed to Lincoln's 1860 victory. On the other hand, good southerners probably had no sympathy for the young barrister who had the audacity to represent that slave Dred Scott before the United States Supreme Court.[32] Just then as though on cue, Father straggled in and was greeted effusively by Mother and me. He was proud to say that he helped save the city. If future generations experience a similar threat to the city I would hope those in charge display the same manliness and step up again.

---

[32] Montgomery Blair High school still exists in Silver Spring, Maryland, just outside of Washington.

1960s

There were still struggles generally in the South between blacks and whites over the issue of civil rights as promised by the Constitution.

On a Sunday in June 1963, I observed a sad ceremony at the old 1894 church on Fourteenth Street NW. This event was on the occasion of the assassination of a stalwart of the civil rights movement named Medgar Evers. The congregation consisted largely of black folks of some means dressed fashionably and having arrived at the church in top-of-the-line automobiles. My parents were certainly counted in that number, all except for the fancy car. It took some persuasion by Mom to get Dad to obtain a more fashionable car in lieu of the now-antiquated 1954 Chevy. Notwithstanding that, their presentation still was much more favorable than that of the less-fortunate members of our race, who gazed longingly at their more opulent brethren inside the church.

1860s

During the day between April 9 and 12, 1865, there was a steady cacophony of church bells ringing commemorating the end of that terrible war. These sounds emanated from the New York Avenue Presbyterian Church, which usually saw the president in attendance, St. Patrick's Cathedral on F Street N, Metropolitan Baptist Church on M Street N, where I would sometimes see Mr. Douglass and people from many other churches. While we now lived several miles north of the city, these bells could be clearly heard from our house, especially if carried on a spring breeze. If one was in Washington city at night, the sounds were intermingled with loud, raucous laughter, shouting, and all other manner of celebration, despite the sometimes chilly and wet spring weather.

During those early days of April 1865, it appeared that nothing could quell the ecstatic atmosphere in the city of Washington. This was the case for white folks as well as us black folks. What the president had often referred to as the "great national nightmare" was finally over. Despite the celebratory mood, life went on as usual in the capital. I was now thirteen and old enough to help with household chores. But a calamitous event beyond comprehension was impending but unbeknownst to us. As it turns out, the famous actor that I would see in Gautier's, the rascal that was Sousa's neighbor along with the rodent-like character who was dining with the actor, were up to a significant mischief that very week. It was Good Friday night, and from our remove in Brightwood, we could hear and see the celebration in Washington City, which included rockets until it abruptly stopped around ten o'clock in the evening. I took pride in confirming a concept that I had learned at the school. Specifically, the fact that we could see the rockets as they were launched down in Washington

City and then a few seconds later hear the attendant explosion proved conclusively that light travels faster than sound.

Curiosity got the better of Father to the point that he placed me in a carriage, and we took the Fourteenth Street road into the city. At around G Street N, our ears were greeted by shouts, sobs, and all manner of emotional and vociferous ejaculations as though some awful event had taken place. When we got near F Street N and Ninth Street W, we encountered a free woman of color, Miss Mary Jane Anderson, one of many of the alley dwellers who lived in Baptist Alley behind Ford's Theatre. She was not sure exactly what had happened, but she related how earlier that evening she saw a very handsome man ride his horse past her house toward the rear of the theatre. She gazed at him "right wishful," she said. She then heard the man cry out, "Ned Spangler." Then a black man by the name of Miles relayed to this "Spangler," "Booth is calling for you." Apparently both Miles and Spangler were stagehands at the theatre because shortly thereafter, "Spangler came and held this 'Booth's' horse for a while while he went into the theatre's rear door." Miss Mary then related her puzzlement when she just saw this Booth rush out of the alley on that same horse at breakneck speed just a few minutes before Father and I encountered her. As we suspected, indeed something terrible had happened. Then, her neighbor Miss Mary Ann Turner, also black, said, "The president has been shot. I believe by that fellow what just rode up the alley."

The April 15 edition of the *National Intelligencer* captioned the event as follows:

Conspiracy and Murder
The President Assassinated
Attempt to Murder Mr. Seward
The Assassins Not Arrested, but Believed Known

Oh how I felt sorry for little Tad Lincoln, a boy of my age, to learn that while watching *Aladdin or His Wonderful Lamp* at Grover's Theatre those aforementioned rascals had conspired to kill his father just around the corner at Ford's Theatre. I could only reflect on how I would feel had it been my father. All throughout that dreadful night, chaos reigned in the streets. Rumors abounded: "General Grant and the entire cabinet have been murdered." "Damn the Rebels. This is their work," said US Marshal for the District of Columbia, Ward Hill Lamon. Indeed, a murderous plot had been afoot. Somewhere in the chaos, I got separated from Father and found myself further west along F Street, where I saw a black man on foot chasing a man on horseback up Vermont Avenue, shouting, "Murder, Murder." As it turned out, that was the servant of Secretary of State Seward, who was in hot pursuit of a who that had just knifed the secretary in his sick chamber.

"What next?" I wondered.

The streets were a virtual madhouse, with every police officer in the four-year-old Metropolitan Police Department on duty and every theatre and saloon closed by the mayor. Father had remained in the neighborhood of the theatre and witnessed the president being carried from that place to a boarding house owned by a tailor named Peterson. He was among thousands who lingered in the streets.

It rained the following day, and despite the downpour, the streets were still packed, especially around that tailor's house. This was right up until 7:22 a.m. Saturday morning, when it was announced that the president had died. Those who had inexplicably slept through this chaotic night would have soon realized that something unusual had occurred because of a strange occurrence. Though dawn had broken, the gaslights in the streets were still on. That was the case of Mrs. Elizabeth Keckley, who was the black dressmaker for Mrs. Lincoln. From her house on Twelfth Street W, she noticed this strange phenomenon, which prompted her to make inquiries. It was in this manner that she learned two things: the awful events of the past evening and that Mrs. Lincoln had called for her for comfort that night. Bells tolled throughout the city, the gloomy, rainy weather complementing the mournful sound of the bells excellently. The city was in mourning for weeks.

On that Easter Sunday, Father Abraham did not rise, Christlike, though he had been slain on Good Friday. His body lay in the East Room of the White House. We, along with thousands of mourners, were resigned to see what we could see from the street. The only other alternative was to stand in the mile-long line that formed near the old canal, winding its way to the southern side of the White House. We had our chance that Wednesday, however, when, despite the entrance of over one hundred thousand people into the city, we were able to witness the funeral procession down the avenue to the capitol. Visitors slept in hotel lobbies, on the streets, and in their carriages.[33]

Some thirty to forty thousand marchers took up the entire one-and-a-half-mile distance between the White House and the capitol. Proudly, Father pointed out that the parade was led by the Twenty-Second United States Colored Infantry that had performed excellent duty during the late unpleasantness in several battles. They would later actually guard some of the perpetrators of this horrible deed after they were sentenced to prison following a trial. We were part of the throng that filed through the rotunda of the capitol to see the flag-draped coffin of the fallen leader. It lay on the catafalque on which, doubtless, a great future assassinated president would lay.

We were among thousands who had lined up more than a mile for a final glimpse at our fallen leader. Side by side walked the "refined and cultured" with the "poor untutored and lately emancipated slaves, each seemingly oblivious to the other." Upon reaching the coffin "some wept and kissed" it.[34]

The news for the next few weeks was dominated by progress in the pursuit and apprehension of the perpetrators of this dastardly deed. It soon became clear that it was not just this Booth who was involved, as Secretary of State Seward was also attacked and Vice President Johnson narrowly escaped becoming a victim. By and by, those responsible were gradually brought to justice. Booth was caught in Virginia, and one Lewis Paine and one George Atzerodt were also captured and charged with conspiracy to kill Seward and Johnson respectively. The word was that Booth was killed in a standoff in the barn of a farmer near Bowling Green in Virginia. But he was not alone. A young companion had surrendered promptly when members of a New York Cavalry unit surrounded the barn. He emerged from the barn, wildly proclaiming his innocence. As it were, it was none other than that mischievous boy who lived near the Navy Yard that Mr. Withers had told me about. I knew that I would hear about him later under

---

[33] Martin S. Nowak, *The White House in Mourning* (London: McFarland and Company, Inc., 2010).

[34] Michael Kauffman, *American Brutus* (New York: Random House, 2004).

other-than-flattering circumstances. Yes, David Herold, the only boy in a sibship of eight, was in serious trouble.

By late April 1865, all culprits had been caught. The word was that they would all be kept aboard two ships at the Navy Yard until taken to the arsenal penitentiary for trial. Crittenden and I were among the throng that crowded the Navy Yard dock to see the accused brought from their holds in the two monitors, the *Saugus* and the *Montauk*. This must have been particularly mortifying for young Davy as he emerged in chains literally into his neighborhood face-to-face with most of his longtime neighbors.

Starting on May 4, the trial of eight conspirators took place. Amid much controversy, it was conducted as a military tribunal notwithstanding the fact that all accused were civilians. The trial in the hot, sweltering courtroom on the third floor of the penitentiary building was destined to last until June 30. The galleries were packed by those lucky enough to gain permission for admission. Many were curious about one particular defendant, Mrs. Mary E. Surratt. She was the owner of a boardinghouse on H Street N. Though it was not one of the aforementioned seedy ones, it was said that those involved in the foul plot met there to plan the crime. Ultimately, she and all of the rest were found guilty. She, along with Paine, Atzerodt, and young Davy, were sentenced to die.

On the morning of July 7, it was ninety degrees before 8:00 a.m. The papers reported a sad procession around noon from the prison cells to the prison yard, where a scaffold for four had been hastily constructed. The four were marched past their coffins and their freshly dug graves to the scaffold. Even if they could have slept the nights since they were told of their guilty findings, it would have been interrupted by the fireworks in the city on the fourth and the sawing and hammering of their death instruments for the past few days and nights. In time, all was ready. One could hear General Winfield Scott Hancock clap his hands twice, and the supports were kicked out from under the platform. Soon four bodies dropped into eternity, displaying an eerie sight as Mrs. Surratt's head leaned at an ominous angle as soon, even with the hood over her head.

1960s

I had just turned twelve in November 1963. Our life in Brightwood, which had once been farmland in Washington County, now part of the city of Washington, was comfortable. Mom continued to remind me of how lucky I was not to share the plight of the less fortunate of our race who were denizens of such places as Anacostia, Congress Heights, or Deanwood. Though we lived several miles north of downtown, we could quickly negotiate a journey by way of streetcar, bus, or car. An interesting phenomenon would come to my attention each July 4, which was consistent with the teachings of my seventh-grade science class. The celebration of the nation's independence on that day featured a televised fireworks display for the occasion that were set off at the Washington Monument grounds some five miles south of us. With the television sound down, we would see each burst of fireworks as they were detonated. We would then wait few seconds and hear the explosion that attended the burst, thus proving conclusively that light travels faster than sound! Unfortunately, school was out for the summer, so I was not able garner extra academic credit for such an astute scientific observation!

All seemed right with the world of a twelve-year-old when on a gorgeous fall Friday, we were shocked to learn that President Kennedy had been shot while riding in a motorcade in Dallas. His children were here in Washington, and oh, how I felt sorry for Caroline and John Jr., who were five and three, respectively. I could only imagine how I would feel had it been my dad. It rained the following day, and the city was in mourning for weeks. We, along with thousands of mourners, filed through the rotunda of the capitol to see the flag-draped coffin of the fallen leader lying on the catafalque on which a great previous assassinated president had lain. Like the assassin of that great previous president who was elected exactly one hundred years before him and tragically killed, this president's assassin was killed before being brought to trial. Unlike that great previous president, no lengthy trial was had. He now also belonged to the ages.

Conclusion

1860s

I can say that for all practical purposes, with the vivid memory of those tragic times in the spring of 1865, my early childhood had concluded. After that, I took on the attitude, ambition, and responsibility of an adult. Residual memories of a childhood in a historic city featuring historic events will remain with me forever. Perhaps similar experiences will be had in this same city in another lifetime.

1960s

I can say that for all practical purposes, my early childhood had concluded in the fall of 1963. Henceforward, I took on the attitude, ambition, and responsibility of an adult. Residual memories of a childhood in an historic city featuring historic events will remain with me forever. But as time went by and I further reflected on these events, it seemed eerily as though this had not been the first time I had experienced coming of age in my hometown of Washington. Perhaps I experienced it in a previous lifetime.